NAVIGATION HISTORY, APPLICATION AND FUN WITH THE SUN

JAMES B. READ

NAVIGATION HISTORY, APPLICATION AND FUN WITH THE SUN

iUniverse books may be ordered through booksellers or by contacting:

iUniverse
1663 Liberty Drive
Bloomington, IN 47403
www.iuniverse.com
844-349-9409

ISBN: 978-1-6632-4736-0 (sc)
ISBN: 978-1-6632-4737-7 (e)

Print information available on the last page.

iUniverse rev. date: 02/03/2023

DEDICATION

I dedicate this book to my friend, neighbor and fellow sailor, Eric Moeller

ACKNOWLEDGEMENTS

My thanks first go to my scientist friend, neighbor and fellow sailor, Eric Moeller. What a perfect situation, me, the instructor and Eric, an eager student with a strong desire to acquire the information that I was presenting. Eric kept asking difficult questions as we went through the drawings and manuscript. The result from his feedback required me to restate or clarify many things and add labels to the drawings. The result of his feedback was that in the end, this document was forced to become clearer and more easily understandable. When I was finished, Eric completely comprehended the material.

My thanks also go to my wife Ann, who took the center cover photo and my picture on the back cover.

INTRODUCTION

This book is the result of much frustration. I had a very difficult time with "HOW TO" navigation books, particularly the ones that attempted to simplify things with rote memory. I would follow along with the exercises but would then become lost, not knowing where I was, or become unable to make sense of what I was reading. Eventually I was able to construct diagrams which I could easily understand and which greatly simplified things for me. Using my diagrams, things became much clearer. The result is what I believe to be a more understandable presentation. Once you comprehend what I have presented, you will be much more able to understand the more detailed material of the EXPERTS.

During the above process, I realized that a short history of navigation would be both interesting and useful. For details of the early explorers, I refer the reader to my previous book: "CURIOSITY, ADVENTURE TRAVEL, EXPLORATION, TRADE, WAR, MURDER".

Finally, it came to me that creation of a sundial which not only can be set for accurate time, but is also capable of plotting the figure 8 ANALEEMA, would also be useful. It would not just be fun, but would increase the reader's understanding of the seasons and make further use of the NAUTICAL ALMANAC.

CHAPTER 1

NAVAGATION HISTORY

Prince Henrique of Portugal, directed the world's first offshore expeditions with the goal of rounding the capes of Africa and reaching India, Japan and the spice Islands. Born Henrique Infante, 1394, he was the third son of King Joao (John). Henry was the recipient of the finest education available and he became an avid reader. His brother had obtained a copy of Rusticello's *IL Millione*, a record of Marco Polos amazing travels and adventures. Henry devoured this book, especially Marco Polo's claims of unlimited gold, spices and other treasures. With virtually no chance of outliving his brothers to become a king himself and, combined with his hatred of Muslims, plus his newly aroused greed, Henry conceived a plan to kill or convert Muslims to Christianity while taking over their trade routes for himself and Portugal.

To develop his master plan and provide a secure site to operate a navigational THINK TANK and or a NAVAGATIONAL SCHOOL, Henry built a secure fortress. The site selection was an easy decision. The limestone cliffs of the Sagres promontory rise vertically, 50 meters above the wild Atlantic. The peninsula is 1,000 meters long and just 200 meters wide where it joins the continent. It is conveniently located, just 15 miles north of the port city of Lagos. To secure the site as a fortress required building only one wall. To staff this operation Henry hired the finest available astronomers, scientists, instrument makers, ship designers and craftsman, even if they were Muslim or Jewish.

Under Henry's direction, circa 1443, the Caravel was created. The Caravel incorporated the world's first ever, stern mounted rudder. The early rudder design mounted a stern facing tiller controlled with lines and blocks (ropes and pulleys). It had two masts, each with a top spar which could be rigged horizontally with square sails for downwind performance, or with one spar end tied down forward, to create a triangular lateen rig. The lateen configuration, with the excess sail reefed, enabled the Caravel to beat upwind just like a modern sailboat. The design was light and swift with a shallow draught to reduce grounding.

Each expedition down the African coast was directed to gather detailed information and create charts of the coastline. Equally important was the collection of weather and wind patterns. Eventually the wind data, detailing direction and velocity for specific locations by date, enabled Henry's scientists to chart and understand the mysterious air flow of the Atlantic.

Early exploration made use of the magnetic compass, invented by the Chinese and disclosed to Europeans by Marco Polo. Henry's instrument makers were tasked with making improvements to enable easy and reliable use. Most likely the Portuguese compass was weighted underneath and suspended on gimbals to keep it level in a seaway and thus preventing the needle from sticking.

In combination with the compass for direction, navigators needed to make rate x time = distance calculations for dead reckoning of their position. Boat speed was determined by throwing a log, attached to a line, from the bow, and estimating speed from the elapsed time to clear the stern. In 2013, while visiting the Columbus Museum at Palos De La Frontera, near Huelva, Spain, I saw a small device consisting of tiny hourglasses mounted on a strip of wood. I returned in 2019 to take a photo but it was no longer on display.

I believe this device, which I call the MEDIEVEL STOPWATCH, was invented by Henry's scientists. This ganged hourglass assembly, consists of six tiny hour glasses mounted on a strip of wood, each containing slightly more sand than the previous one. Created for easy and accurate timing of boat speed and accompanied with a pre-calculated chart, log time in seconds can be immediately converted to boat speed.

For example, six nautical miles per hour is very close to 10 ft. /sec. If a nautical mile (nm), is rounded down from 6080 to 6000 feet as does the U.S. Navy, where a nm = 2000 yards, it is precisely 10 feet/ second. Six knots = 6 x 6000 = 36,000 ft./hr. One hour = 60 minutes or 3,600 sec. 36,000 divided by 3,600 = 10 / 1 or 10 ft. / sec.

A log would pass a 90- foot caravel traveling 6 nm / HR in 9 seconds. 18 seconds = 3nm / HR, 54 seconds = 1 nm / HR, (drifting). The practical range of the instrument is 5.4 seconds for 10 nm / HR and 27 seconds for 2 nm / HR. The hourglass strip is inverted for the 54 second timeout. Speed in nautical miles (knots) is usually indicated by K.

Math logic

1 K = 54 sec.	three x 3K time (1K=one nautical mile =6080 feet)
2 K = 27 sec.	1/2 x 1K time (One statute mile = 5,280 feet)
3 K = 18 sec.	twice ref time
4 K = 13.5 sec.	1/2 x 2K time
5 K = 10.8 sec.	twice 10K time
6 K = 9 sec (reference time)	
7 K = 7.7 sec.	1/7 x 1K time
8 K = 6.75 sec.	1/4 x 2K time
9 K = 6 sec.	1/3 x 3K time
10 K = 5.4 sec.	1/10 x 1K time

If I was determining the six sand timeouts, I would set it up in seconds as follows: 6, 9, 10.8, 13.5, 18, 27. What clever people these Portuguese, the pilot had exact boat speed as soon as the log cleared the stern.

The next navigational problem is LATITUDE DETERMINATION. Henry's scientists were still working on this in 1460 when Henry died. They had improved astrolabe performance and developed the cross staff for more accurate measurement of the sun angle to the horizon. The astronomers were attempting to create an EPHEMERIS, a NAUTICAL ALMANAC listing the sun's position for each day of the year. With no funds available to continue, the scientists abandoned the project. Without Henry's sponsorship the expeditions languished and virtually ceased.

In 1481, Henry's grand- nephew, became King Joao II (John II). After solidifying his power base by dispatching two dissenting relatives, the new king resumed Henry's grand plan and restarted work on the ephemeris.

High atop Lisbon on the roof of Castello St George, the scientists created a device to measure the elevation of the sun (FIG.10)). This consisted of a wooden pole, mounted on east / west bearings, with gunsight type sights mounted on each end. Lenses would not be invented until the next century. Attached was a marker which indicated the resulting angle. This pole could only swing a north / south arc. The goal was to measure the maximum angle of the sun as it crossed the MERIDIAN at the ZENITH (highest point in the sky). The MERIDIAN is a longitude which is part of a great circle that passes through both the north and south poles.

Each clear day, the angle was measured and listed in a book. After five years of collecting this data, the ephemeris was complete. The latitude of Lisbon was known. The sun's seasonal movement, 23.5 degrees north and south had been known by the ancients. Now with the newly measured angular data, the GP (geographical position of the sun on the surface of the earth, center to center) could be tabulated in reference to the equator for each day of the year. In other words, the latitude of the sun was listed for each day of the year. If the pilot knew the GP of the sun in reference to the equator and could measure his distance to the GP then he was able to determine his latitude. Exactly how this is achieved will be covered in great detail later.

This single achievement, the ability to determine LATITUDE AT SEA, became available to King John's pilots by 1486. It literally opened up the world for navigation and was the KEY which enabled all future seaborne exploration.

In 1488, Bartolomeu Dias, now able to determine his latitude and making use of newly acquired wind data, crossed the equator while nearly touching Brazil. He continued counterclockwise, downwind on the South Atlantic, finally rounding both capes of Africa.

In 1492, Columbus, in possession of this STATE SECRET, managed to discover the new world. On his fourth trip to the new world, making use of the almanac's data to predict an eclipse, he was able to persuade a Caribbean chief that he possessed magical power and could take away the sun. When the moon began nibbling away at the sun's edge, the distraught chief gladly provided the provisions that had previously been denied Columbus, if only he would restore the sun.

In 1496, Vasco De Gama, making use of the data collected by Dias, cut the time to the capes in half. He continued halfway up the east coast of Africa then heading east, made landfall at the real India.

In 1524, the Magellan expedition, enlightened with the new discovery that the Pacific Ocean lay beyond Panama (Balboa), completed the world's first circum-navigation.

IMAGINE, just with the ability to master this new technique, enabling pilots to know their LATITUDE, the ENTIRE WORLD became revealed, all in the space of a SINGLE LIFETIME. For instance, I am 80 years of age. If I had been born in 1450, ten years before Henry's passing, I could have witnessed it all. I would have been 10 years old when Henry died, 31 when John became king, 50 at the turn of the century, and just 74 when the **VICTORIA** *completed her circum-navigation and returned to Seville.*

CHAPTER 2

LATITUDE DETERMINATION

The relationship of one's latitude to the equator is a THREE-PART EQUATION. The three parts are: The OBSERVER'S LATITUDE, the GP, geographical position of the SUN or other heavenly body, and distance from the GP to the EQUATOR, (determined from the ALMANAC). With knowledge of two parts, the third is easily determined. In order to simplify things, let us go back in time before Magellan and Eratosthenes to FLATLAND, when the known earth was still FLAT.

On 1 AUG, 2019, I measure the angle from the horizon to the sun as it crosses my MERIDIAN (at ZENITH, its position highest in the sky). MERIDIANS of longitude are GREAT CIRCLES that pass through both poles. Therefor when on my meridian, the sun will be either directly north, overhead, or directly south. I know my location to be approximately, 38N. With my sextant, I measure the angle between the SUN and the HORIZON to be 70 degrees. I construct a right triangle with a line from my position, 70 degrees from the horizon to the sun (FIG. 01). The horizon forms the baseline. I drop a vertical line from the sun to the baseline (90 degrees to the base). The line connecting the center of the sun with the center of the earth, passes through the earth's surface at a point named the GP (geographical position). More detail on the GP later.

The complementary angle of 70 is 20 degrees. This is the ARC DISTANCE between me, the observer and the sun's GP. Therefore, the sun is 20 degrees to my south. From the almanac I determine that the sun is 18 degrees north of the equator at 18N. If the sun is 18 degrees north of the equator and I am 20 degrees north of the sun, my position must be 18 + 20 = 38N.

The second example is virtually the same as the first except this time the sun is in the southern hemisphere. On 1 JAN, 2019, I measure the angle of the sun to the horizon to be 29 degrees (FIG. 02). Using the same technique as on the first example, the GP of the sun is 90 – 29 = 61 degrees from my location. On 1 JAN, the almanac lists the sun as 23S. In order to determine my latitude, I must subtract 23 degrees from the GP to find my distance to the equator. 61 – 23 = 38N, my exact latitude. I have selected the dates which list full degrees to explain the CONCEPT most simply. Later I will use sextant examples which will show more PRECISION.

Now to show the science which enables us to allow the simplification above.

Please refer to (FIG. 03). The FLATLAND simplification is illustrated with a level line tangent to a circle which represents the earth. The observer is standing on the FLATLINE line and is tangent, directly above the earth's center.

Dropping down to the next illustration, the FLATLINE is shifted to the left and the GP is now tangent above the center of the earth. We can justify this because the all the sun's rays are parallel.

The sun's rays are parallel because the trigonometric ratio of the two sides of the representative triangle is effectively zero. The distance between the earth and sun is 93,000,000 miles. The radius of the earth is 4,000 miles. This can be represented by a right triangle with a side 1-mile long, the other being 23,250 miles. The included angle is so tiny as to be virtually- unmeasurable, hence parallel.

In the lowest Illustration, The FLATLINE is wrapped around the circle representing the earth and now conforms to a real-world view.

The FLATLAND latitude determination triangles are only possible when the sun is directly overhead on the MERIDIAN (FIG. 04). At this single moment in time there exist only TWO possible positions, YOURS, WHERE YOU ARE STANDING, and the OTHER, FAR AWAY, but on the same great circle with the same angle to the sun. The observer will know his approximate latitude and the hemisphere in which he is located. The other position obviously makes no sense.

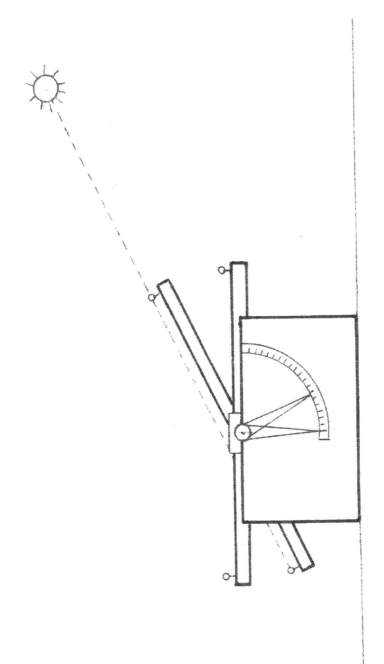

AUTHOR'S VERSION,
JOAO II OBSERVATORY

FIG. 00

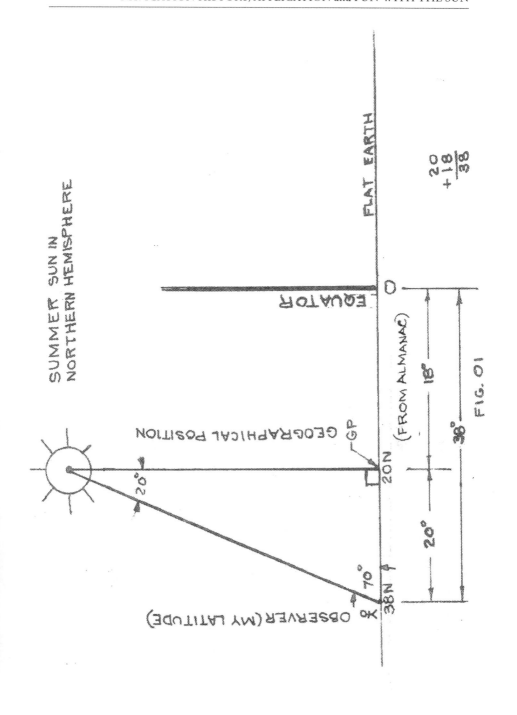

FIG. 01

$$\begin{array}{r} 20 \\ +18 \\ \hline 38 \end{array}$$

SUMMER SUN IN NORTHERN HEMISPHERE

FLAT EARTH

EQUATOR

GEOGRAPHICAL POSITION

GP

20N

(FROM ALMANAC)

18°

38°

20°

70°

38N

OBSERVER (MY LATITUDE)

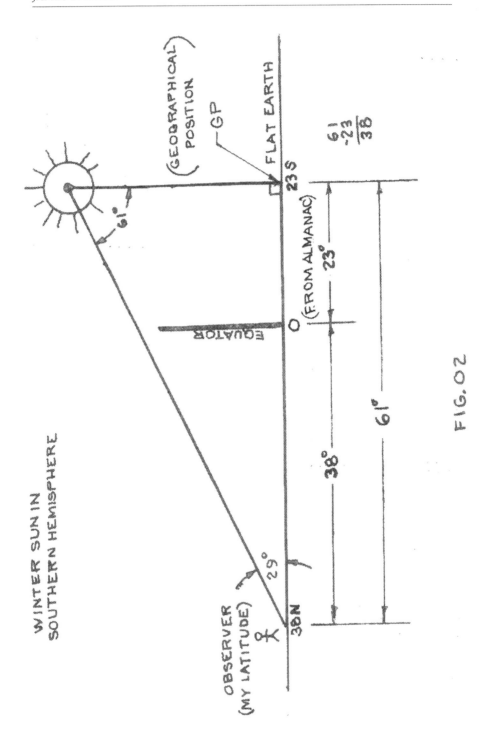

WINTER SUN IN
SOUTHERN HEMISPHERE.

OBSERVER
(MY LATITUDE)

29°

38N

EQUATOR

O

(FROM ALMANAC)

23°

61°

(GEOGRAPHICAL
POSITION)

GP

FLAT EARTH

23 S

38°

61°

$$\begin{array}{r} 61 \\ -23 \\ \hline 38 \end{array}$$

FIG. O2

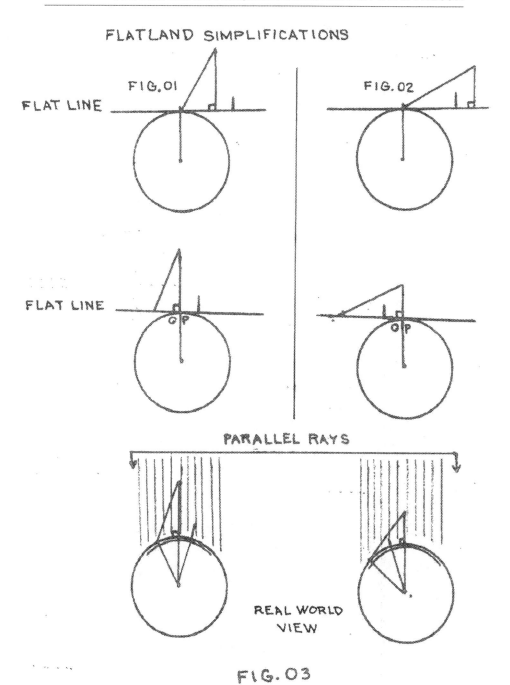

FLATLAND SIMPLIFICATIONS

FLAT LINE   FIG.01

FIG.02

FLAT LINE

PARALLEL RAYS

REAL WORLD
VIEW

FIG.03

CHAPTER 3

LONGITUDE DETERMINATION

Longitude is slightly more complicated because the distance between meridians varies with latitude and precise measurement requires a precision time comparison with Greenwich, England.

Early pilots knew the approximate circumference of the earth based on the experiment by Eratosthenes, long before the birth of Christ. This experiment, performed in Alexandria, Egypt with a simple stick, represents the highest analytical ability of the human brain, on a level with Isaac Newton and Albert Einstein. He measured the shadow angle of a vertical stick to be 1/ 50th of a circle (7.2 degrees) on the summer solstice, 21 JUN. He knew that on that day in Aswan, (located virtually due north of Alexandria), the shadow of a man's head would block the sunlight from reaching the bottom of a well. In other words, a stick would cast no shadow. Aswan lies very close to the TROPIC OF CANCER, 23.5N. If the distance between Alexandria, his location, and Aswan, directly to the north was known, the circumference of the earth would equal 50 times that. He calculated the distance by averaging records of camel caravan transit times between the two cities. Amazingly, the circumference value he obtained was within 10% of the actual 25,251 STATUTE MILE distance, measured at sea level.

A STATUTE MILE measures 5,280 feet. A NAUTICAL MILE measures 6,080 feet. The nm is by definition: 1/60th of a degree. 1 nm multiplied by 60 x 360 degrees = 21,600 nm which is exactly equal to the 25,251-statute mile circumference.

One degree of LATITUDE is always 60 nm, anywhere between the north and south poles. One degree of LONGITUDE is 60 nautical miles ONLY at the equator. At any other latitude it must be shortened by the COSINE of the adjacent latitude. A longitudinal line is by definition: a MERIDIAN which passes through the north and south poles. The spacing between lines varies from a maximum of 60 miles at the equator to a single point, ZERO, at the poles.

Before proceeding, let us understand what the COSINE means. The COSINE, abbreviated "cos" is a trigonometry function and is a ratio between two sides and the included angle of a 90-degree triangle. The maximum value is ONE, the minimum value is ZERO. The cos table lists ratios which are based on corresponding included angles. The longest side which is always opposite the 90-degree angle is named the HYPOTENUSE and will carry the value of 60 nm. The other side of the included angle (which denotes the cos of the LATITUDE) represents the foreshortened LONGITUDE.

The way this operates is simply a reduction of the full 60 nm based on the chosen latitude to determine the resultant longitude. In other words, the 60 nm is simply multiplied by the listed cos value for that latitude. Each increasing degree of latitude foreshortens the 60-mile base by the trigonometric cosine function. At 60 degrees the distance is 30 miles and at 90 it is 0. The math is ultra-simple, just multiply the 60-mile equator distance by the cosine. This is ultra-simple, please don't let the word trigonometry bully or frighten you, the TRIG RESULT IS JUST A MULTIPLIER. Refer to the table (FIG. 05)

All early pilots understood this relationship and used it in their distance estimates as total longitude distance could only be estimated. A relatively certain method used to find a known destination was to sail down (along) their latitude while using rate x time = distance calcs (Columbus method).

One method, which is complicated, but can be used all but 6 days of the month, is the LUNAR DISTANCE method. Greenwich astronomers created an almanac listing the position of the moon for a 23-year cycle. They also listed the positions of certain background stars plus the position of the sun. The navigator was required to measure the altitude of the moon, plus the distance to the celestial comparison body, the angular distance between them. This method required a clock (unreliable at sea as a precision measuring device) plus a long string of calculations. During the middle 1700's, the sextant was still under development, few navigators were able to make the required measurements. It is interesting to note that the world's first single handed circumnavigation was completed by Joshua Slocum circa 1900. Slocum, a former clipper ship captain successfully used the lunar distance method, plus noon sights, all timed with a simple alarm clock.

THE LONGITITUDE ACT

Following a series of shipwreck disasters, Parliament passed the LONGITUDE ACT of 1714. The prize was 20, 000 pounds, a multi-million-dollar fortune by today's measure. It would be paid to the first person, who's method would enable a navigator to determine his longitude within one half of a degree, 30 miles or less. The Longitude Committee, composed primarily of mathematicians and astronomers, such as Isaac Newton and Edmond Halley, was tasked with the final determination.

The clocklike earth makes a full rotation once every 24 hours. This amounts to one degree every 4 minutes or 15 degrees per hour. Thus, if a precision timepiece, unaffected by either temperature or the motion of the sea could be constructed, it would enable a navigator to compare his local time with the time at a fixed reference meridian, (Greenwich), and thusly DETERMINE his longitude. Newton did not believe such a timepiece could be constructed but definitely approved of the concept. The two competing methods, the CLOCKLIKE EARTH and the LUNAR DISTANCE method were developed simultaneously.

Astronomers pursued the lunar distance method where the MOON'S position could be compared to either the sun, planets or background stars. The Astronomer Royal, John Flamsteed, working in the newly constructed Greenwich Observatory began timing and logging the transit of the sun, moon, Jupiter, Venus, Saturn, Mars, and 57 navigational reference stars. This data was tabulated in an almanac.

The star motion turned out to be relatively easy to track. In the space of a year, the relationship of the stars to each other is essentially constant. This is long before Edwin Hubbel discovered the expanding universe. For navigational purpose, the stars positions are fixed over a one-year period.

The entire group is referenced to the "FIRST POINT OF ARIES" the Ram. When I first was explained this concept, I thought, how difficult this must be? The reality is quite simple, it is the point in time when the northbound sun crosses the equator, the first moment of the VERNAL EQUINOX.

The motion of the moon and planets to each other took much longer to understand and was still being updated and revised up to and beyond the time when the prize was awarded to a watch and clockmaker. Accurate tables for comparison of these bodies were developed over decades, with input from both the U.S. Naval Observatory and the Greenwich Observatory.

MEASUREMENT

Equally important as the tabulated data collection, was the development of an instrument to make precision measurements. The cross-staff with four available inserts was an improvement over the astrolabe. The back-staff came next, allowing the navigator to place his back to the sun. Many early navigators were blind in one eye from sun damage. As necessity is the mother of invention and with the urgent requirement of making precision measurements, two inventors created a nearly identical design almost simultaneously. In 1732, American inventor Thomas Godfrey and vice president of the Royal Society, John Hadley, each independently created a design for the Octant. This device, measuring 1/8 of a circle and using two mirrors could split the horizon with an image of the surface on the left side and the celestial object on the right. The object image is brought down to touch the horizon and the angle is displayed on the lower surface of the frame. Jesse Ramsden, an English instrument maker, created the modern design known as a Sextant. It expanded the scale to 1/6 of a circle and is capable of measuring angles up to 120 degrees for making horizontal distance comparisons. A worm drive, acting against very precision cut gear teeth, rotates a full turn for each measured degree. This manufacturing process is known as ENGINE DIVIDING. The knob for the worm drive has a Vernier scale allowing measurements to within 1/30 of a degree or 2 arc seconds. Before taking a reading, the instrument is adjusted to zero degrees: The two images are compared and adjusted for a level horizon. The scale is re-examined, and any difference is noted as INSTRUMENT ERROR. The brass frame, subject to thermal expansion, is always changing, therefore small deviations are expected and are noted as Ie.

TIME MEASUREMENT

John Harrison (1693-1776). Always a precision craftsman, began his career as a carpenter and joiner. Fascinated with clocks he began building them from a variety of different wood. The wooden gears were a composite, selected for grain structure and he even incorporated an oily wood, lignum vitae, to reduce friction. As his skill progressed, he began experimenting with a way to maintain exact pendulum length, a longer pendulum slows down the clock, a shorter one speeds it up. To compensate for temperature changes, he determined that by interconnecting different lengths of steel and brass rods, he could resolve this problem. Temperature compensation in clock and watch motion would dominate his creative thinking, eventually enabling him to win the longitude prize. To evaluate performance, he would measure a star on successive nights as it disappeared behind a wall.

The night sky, tracking as SIDERAL time, moves faster than the 24-hour solar day, the difference being 3 minutes, 56 seconds. The cause of this phenomena is the earth's yearly orbit around the sun. The product of this nearly four-minute loss, times 366 equals a complete solar year, 365.242 days.

Harrison would note the time as he listened to the tick tock sound of the escapement wheel, all while leaning out his window and watching the object star disappear behind a building. This method allowed him to evaluate his pendulum changes in real time. His long case clocks eventually became known as REGULATORS. When he became aware of the LONGITITUDE PRIZE, he dedicated the rest of his life to its solution.

His first chronometer which became known as H1, took 5 years to construct. Made entirely of brass, it incorporates two double ended pendulums, mounted in the same plane and which swing in opposite directions. This huge time machine will barely fit inside a 9 cubic foot enclosure and looks like something from a science fiction movie. The

Greenwich Observatory museum has cleaned and polished it and placed it on display where any curious visitor can view it in dazzling motion.

Harrison became seasick while accompanying H1 on a 1736 sea trial to Lisbon and back to London. The clock fared much better, allowing the longitude to actually be kept within 30 miles, at all times. He was commissioned to produce another time piece known as H2, completed in 1739. Unsatisfied with H2, he embarked on a third timepiece, completed 19 years later. In 1760, Harrison presented the Board of Longitude with H3, ready for sea trials. During the meeting, he revealed the little beauty that would eventually capture the prize.

H4, a 5-inch oversize pocket watch, incorporated a solid gold spiral balance spring. Temperature compensation was accomplished by attaching a riveted bimetal strip of brass and steel to the balance spring. A ratcheting mechanism was incorporated between the mainspring and the winding fob so that daily winding would not momentarily affect the unit. Diamond bearings were used to reduce friction. After two years of tweaking, he presented it to the Board. In 1762, after a year of evaluation by the Board and a successful sea trial to Jamaica, the Board of Longitude modified the rules of the prize.

Nevil Maskelyne became the 5th Astronomer Royal, and by this position, a member of the Board of Longitude. He was the one who lobbied to have the rules changed. In what was clearly a conflict of interest, he wanted the prize awarded to the Lunar Distance method in which he had an interest.

Harrison produced his final timepiece, known as H5, which he personally presented to King George III. King George had a private observatory and accepted H5 for his personal evaluation. H5 performed flawlessly.

When Harrison became aware of the new prize requirements, he considered this the last straw, he had met the full requirements several times over. A frustrated Harrison re-approached King George III, who declared, "By God! Harrison, I will see you righted"! Parliament eventually awarded him 8,500 pounds for a lifetime total of 22,500.

While H4 met all original requirements, there existed the possibility that it was a fluke and not repeatable. The new rules required that to qualify for the prize, a chronometer must be more rigorously tested, be reproduceable in quantities, and thus be available to shipping. Harrison was directed to release H4 to watchmaker Larcum Kendall for reproduction. Kendall completed K1 in 1769, receiving 500 pounds. He then submitted it to the Greenwich Observatory for testing.

For his second voyage of discovery, Captain James Cook (1728-1779) was issued K1 plus 3 chronometers produced by John Arnold. The secondary mission of the expedition was to rigorously test these devices and prove that copies of H4 were reliable in a seaway and across a wide temperature range. To guarantee the fidelity of testing, the Admiralty commissioned William Wales, a Board of Longitude astronomer, to accompany Cook. The trip lasted 3 years, covering excursions to Antarctica, back and forth through the tropics, and finally returning to England in 1775. Both Cook and Wales had the highest praise for K1, an exact copy of H4. It reportedly did not vary more than 8 seconds in any given day (seems like a lot), always allowing longitude to be kept within 30 miles. The 3 Arnold units were not exact copies and proved inferior to K1.

Following Captain Cook and William Wales' praise of K1 plus the awarding of the LONGITUDE prize to the then 80-year old Harrison, chronometers began to be produced in quantity, and at affordable prices. In modern times, a good quartz watch, maintaining nearly constant temperature from body heat, combined with a daily list of deviation (there will always be a directional gain or loss), can make an excellent chronometer. For correction, time signals are broadcast by both England and America. In the USA, the time signals are transmitted at frequencies of 5, 10, 15, 20, and 25 megahertz from Colorado, WWV, and Hawaii, WWVH

CHAPTER 4

THE NOON SIGHT

In the modern world, commercial ships report their noon position to headquarters. This is a tradition evolved from the noon sight. I will now describe a method of locating a ships position at sea without benefit of GPS or modern technology.

For navigational purposes the earth stands still while the sun revolves around it once every 24 hours. Therefore, every 24 hours the sun does a 360-degree rotation around the earth or 15 degrees per hour. Because England became the world's mightiest maritime power it placed a navigational reference point and observatory at the "center of the world", the Greenwich district of London. The reference point is the zero or Greenwich Meridian which is also a longitude that passes through the north and the south pole. The Greenwich Observatory houses a transit telescope with trunnions on an east/west axis so that it can only swing in a rigid north to south direction. This north/south vertical swing of the telescope enables the observatory to measure the transit or crossing time of any celestial object, i.e the sun, moon, planets or stars at the zero meridian. The definition of a meridian crossing is when an object passes from east to west and is momentarily directly overhead, on a great circle of longitude also known as ZENITH. Making use of repeated daily transit measurements, the observatory creates and publishes the Nautical Almanac.

Because the sun rotates 24 hours per day or 15 degrees per hour, the earth is segmented into 24 equal time zones. Political time zones vary, navigational time zones do not, nor do they allow for political "daylight saving time". With regard to the noon position of the sun in London, the Greenwich meridian was designated to be hour zero. Therefore, hour 0 is located exactly on zero longitude. Exactly half way around world (180 is half of 360) is the 180th meridian or longitude 180. Hour 12 is located on the 180th meridian. The navigational day begins at MIDNIGHT, UT Universal Time in Greenwich. At that same time, it is NOON, 12:00 hours, 00 minutes, in Tonga exactly on the 180th meridian. This is the INTERNATIONAL DATE LINE. Crossing the LINE from the west deletes a day.

I flew from San Francisco to Auckland, New Zealand on Friday, 21 MAY, 2013. An entire day was subtracted from my calendar. The time remained the same but the day became Saturday, 22 MAY. I got the 24 hours back, 1 hour at a time while continuing west. The calendar date is ONE DAY AHEAD of Greenwich, but becomes the same 12 hours later at Greenwich midnight.

GMT, Greenwich Mean Time, the actual time in Greenwich, England is identical to UT, Universal Time. GMT in Tonga, matches Greenwich because the TIME is UNIVERSAL.

GHA, GREENWICH HOUR ANGLE: Longitude on earth begins at the Greenwich or prime meridian (000), located at Greenwich, England. GHA is measured WESTWARD all the way around (360 degrees) to 000. Thus, GHA begins its 24-hour journey at Greenwich NOON and continues its up-count until NOON the next day.

LONGITUDE tracks exactly with GHA all the way to 180E and 180W at which point both are the same. With GHA, increasing westward past 180 degrees, Longitude begins to DECREASE, from 180 back to 000.

When GHA (Greenwich Hour Angle) is listed as 180E. The sun continues moving west as the GHA increases to 359:59.9 near NOON and then then becomes- 000:00.0W at ZENITH on the Greenwich meridian. Longitude can never exceed 180 so you must subtract your GHA from 360 for East longitude. For instance, a boat located 10 hours east of Greenwich will be at longitude 15 x 10 = E 150:00. The GHA for zone 14 is 210. Subtracting 210 from 360 = E150. I hope this is not too confusing but it is what it is.

As anyone who has experimented with a sundial knows, the sun only crosses the local meridian at high noon four times a year. At other times of the year the meridian crossing will be up to 16 minutes early or late. I actually own a small hanging sundial that can be compensated for this variation . This is a crude and early version of a marine chronometer.

The Greenwich Observatory produces an ephemeris titled THE NAUTICAL ALMANAC. For simplicity, I will, for the moment, restrict this discussion of the Nautical Almanac to the sun. Inside this booklet can be found the GHA, Greenwich Hour Angle and the Dec, DECLINATION, (LATITUDE OF THE SUN). GHA zero is the time of the Greenwich meridian crossing of the sun. By comparing the exact time, the sun crosses my meridian with the current GHA time, I can determine my longitude.

On March 20th the sun leaves the southern hemisphere, crossing the equator northbound. This marks the start of SPRING, the VERNAL EQUINOX and the first point of ARIES the ram, the reference that star positions are measured from. At the moment the sun is on the meridian of the equator, its DEC, declination is zero degrees, 00:00.0. The sun continues moving northward for 3 months until it reaches latitude 23 degrees, 26 minutes north, the June 21st SUMMER SOLSTICE. At this time the DEC is 23:26.0N. Continuing this yearly cycle, the sun then reverses and heads south. On reaching the equator September 22nd, which terminates summer, it continues south to the WINTER SOLSTICE on December 21st at DEC 23:26.0S. It then reverses northward to complete the cycle.

LATITUDE is measured in degrees from the equator (0) to the north pole (90N) and from the equator (0) to -90 or (90S). All latitude measurements are equal in distance, that is one degree which measures 60 nm (nautical miles) near the equator is the same near either pole.

LONGITUDE is also measured in degrees, E east or W west. At the equator one degree equals 60 nm. At the north or south pole, all meridians converge to measure zero miles. All distances between the equator and the poles are reduced by the cosine of the latitude (refer to the chart). Charts produced with Mercator projection are compensated to provide a measurable solution of the foreshortened distance. "When measuring distances on a chart, always use the vertical latitude scale.

DISTANCE is measured in nm, nautical miles where, as stated above, one degree equals 60 nm and one nm equals one minute. The circumference of the earth is approximately 25,000 statute miles at 5,280 feet per mile. The circumference of the earth in nm is 60 x 360 which equals 21,600 nm. A nm, 1 / 21,600 equals 6,080 feet. As a matter of interest, the United States Navy rounds a nm down to 2,000 yards for targeting purpose.

SEXTANT MEASURE OF NOON SIGHT

On January 1st, 2016, I attempted to perform a noon sight with supposedly ideal conditions at Drakes Beach on the Point Reyes National Seashore, 25 miles north of San Francisco. The exact location as displayed on a GPS is 38:01.6N by 122:57.4W. The sun was low in the sky and was producing a wide band of reflections. My sextant incorporates a pair of rotating polarized filters. The filter to reduce the blinding effects of the sun was OK. The filter to reduce glare was frozen and refused to rotate. The result was frustrating; my measurements were all over the place because the horizon was fuzzy, not sharp. I threw away my notes but I still could have determined latitude.

On January 1st the Dec of the sun was 23:00S. My latitude was virtually 38:00N. Working backward the sextant reading had to be 29 degrees. The simple math for this problem with the sun south of the equator is: 90 – (23 + sextant reading). 90 - (23 + 29) = 38 =38N.

Many days later I managed to free the stuck filter and prepared for a new attempt.

On Friday, May27th I returned to the exact same location, halfway between the parking lot and the surf, 100 yards from the museum. This time I truly had ideal conditions: The sun was now high in the sky and the horizon was crisp, so crisp that I didn't use the filter. My friend and assistant, Finn, had a clipboard plus my wife's i-phone which displayed the exact time in minutes and seconds in large digital numbers. Unlike taking measurements from a rocking boat and timing the readings for an average eye height I was standing on terra firm. The plan was to take a careful reading, bringing the lower edge of the sun (lower limb) down to the horizon and shout ready then mark when I had what I considered a good reading. He would subtract one second then record the time. I would then read and call out the sextant angle in degrees, minutes and tenths of minutes. The process was repeated until the sun reached maximum height then began descending.

Before going into the readings and corrections let me discuss some details: The sextant measures an angle noted as Hs. The sextant always has an instrument error mostly caused by temperature variation and is noted as Ie. My sextant read PLUS 4 minutes when the reflected image and actual horizon were aligned together. Many navigators would consider this sloppy and when I was actively using the instrument, I kept it adjusted to keep the error under 2 minutes. To correct for this, I must subtract 4 minutes from Hs. The sun and moon each have a diameter of approximately half a degree or 30 minutes. The center of the sun is 15 minutes above the lower limb. The atmosphere acts as a refracting lens, maximizing apparent height at low altitudes with nearly true readings higher than 70 degrees. When you observe a sunset and the upper limb just disappears, it is already far below the horizon.

The altitude correction for the SUN CENTER at this elevation and this time of year is +15.7 minutes. This is from the ALTITUDE CORRECTION TABLES, located in the front of the Nautical Almanac. The TABLE is split, OCT- MAR, and APR-DEC. The earth is closer to the SUN in winter and more distant in summer

The DIP correction is also listed on the Altitude Correction page. The higher above the surface of the earth, the more distant the horizon. The DIP correction must be subtracted from the observer's eye height for the true horizon. The height of my eye while standing comfortably behind the surf line was approximately 8 feet above the level of the water. I disregarded the tide height which also happens to equally affect and balance the surf with the horizon. My horizon was about 2 to 3 miles distant. This is from experience and is later confirmed when Chimney Rock screws up my horizon and the far edge of Drake's Bay becomes my new horizon, without any noticeable affect on the accuracy of my readings.

8 feet of DIP correction listed in a table is -2.8 minutes. The result after all corrections is height observed or Ho. The following are the actual *measurements and corrections:*

Now for the actual readings:
TIME ANGLE
11:48:21 72:39.5
12:00:05 73:11.5
12:05:22 73:13.2
12:06:22 73:17.5*
12:07:23 73:14.5
12:08:08 73:16.0
12:09:15 73:16.0
12:11:05 73:19.0*
12:12:21 73:15.0
12:13:11 73:13.5
12:14:09 73:13.0
12:29:46 72:39.5

Both measurements denoted by an asterisk (*) were obviously wrong and were ignored. They did not fit an otherwise smooth transition. After determining that the sun was descending, I set the instrument to match the 72:39.5 height and timed the reoccurrence. The mid time of the two 72:39.5 readings is 12:09:15 which agrees with the position and spacing of my highest reading. THE SUN CROSSED MY MERIDIAN AT 12:09:15 AT A HEIGHT OF 73:16.0.

Hs 73:16.0	Hs is the actual sextant reading.
Ac +15.7	Ac is the altitude correction for the SUN's center.
Ie -04.0	Ie is the sextant error.
DIP -02.8	DIP is the correction for the horizon.
Ho 73:27	Ho is the corrected result.

Now from the NAUTICAL ALMANAC, FRIDAY MAY 27, 2016:

UT GHA DEC
11:00 345:42.2 N21:24.6
12:00 000:42.1 N21:24.6
20:00 120:41.5 N21:27.9
21:00 135:41.4 N21:28.3

Observing the table, the sun crossed the GREENWICH MERIDIAN sometime between 11 and 12 noon, UT universal time reaching a GHA of 359:59.9 then becoming 000:00.0 at TRANSIT. We do not need to interpolate the time of GHA zero, I only showed it for clarity and to help the reader understand what is represented.

San Francisco (my closest large city) is located in time zone 8, 8 hours west of Greenwich, one third of the way around the world. Because we are inside zone 8, we add 8 hours, my UT begins with hour 20. Note: Political daylight saving time is not allowed in these calcultions,

UT	GHA	DEC
20:00	120:41.5	N21:27.9
00:09:15	02:18.8	N00:00.1
20:09:15	123:00.3	N21:28.0

The 02:18.8 came from a table inside the almanac which gives a between the hour GHA ARC DISTANCE reading for each minute and second of TIME. The 00:00.1 was determined as follows. Between UT 20:00 and UT 21:00 the sun moved north 00.4 minutes or 0.1 minute every 15 minutes of time. I interpolated 09:15 to be closer to 0.1 than zero.

OUR LONGITUDE is 123:00W
OUR LATITUDE is 90 − (73:25 + 21:28) = 38:03N

The GPS indicated N38:01.6 and W122:57.4. Rounding the GPS figures gives N38:02 and W122:57.

When a noon sight is taken at sea on a bouncing rolling vessel, I expect to be within 3 miles of latitude and 20 miles of longitude. Naturally early seafarers could only do latitude before the invention of the chronometer. My guess is that latitude could be determined within a 30-mile range using a cross staff and crude almanac.

CHAPTER 5

NOON SIGHT IN OPPOSITE HEMISPHERE

On 5 FEB,2020 I performed a second noon sight, this time at Limantour beach. This site has a 170 -degree clear horizon to the sea. This proved to be a much more difficult task than the previous one. This time the sun was in the southern hemisphere, much lower in the sky. The arc across the meridian was much flatter. The sea was calm and flat, which caused a thick, fuzzy reflection band. The result was a wide variation in the readings.

In a sense this was a good thing, simulating readings in a rolling, pithing boat. This situation required me to plot the points on a grid, then average the curve between points.

SUNSIGHT 2:
05 FEB, 2020

NOON SIGHT, SUN IN OPPOSITE HEMISPHERE (CONTRARY name to latitude):

Time	Angle (Altitude)(Height)	Time	Angle
12:03:00	35:41.2'	12:20:20	35:54.4'
12:04:29	35:42.0'	12:21:40	35:55.3'
12:05:37	35:41.5'	12:22:43	35:49.9'
12:06:36	35:42.8'	12:24:17	35:53.3'
12:07:58	35:43.2'	12:26:14	35:50.9'
12:10:01	35:47.7'	12:27:26	35:50.1'
12:11:21	35:46'8' *	12:28:36	35:49.1'

12:14:17	35:54.5'	12:29:37	35:50.1'
12:15:27	35:56.5'	12:31:21	35:49.4'
12:17:54	35:55.2'	12:33:01	35:46.5'*
12:19:18	35:56.0'	12:34:07	35:46.3'

This time the sun was in the opposite hemisphere. In 30 minutes of collecting data, the sun stayed within a range of less than half a degree on my sextant. To further increase the difficulty, the sea was very calm but highly reflective, making for a very un-crisp horizon. The result simulated readings from a bouncing, rolling boat and required a plotting sheet to resolve.

From the plot: THE SUN CROSSED MY MERIDIAN AT 12:18:00 AT A HEIGHT OF 35:55.5 DEGREES.

Measured altitude (ANGLE)	Hs 35:55.5'
Altitude (ANGLE) correction, OCT-MAR	Ac +14.9
Instrument error, +0.6	Ie -0.6
Eye height correction, 10'	DIP -3.1
	————
Corrected observation	Ho 35:66.7 = 36:06.7 (minutes cannot exceed 60)

Add 8 hours (zone 8)   TIME 20:18:00
From Almanac, 5 FEB, 2020:

UT (GMT)	GHA	DEC
12	356:30.7'	S15:59.8'
13	011:0.7'	S15:59.1'
20	116:30.3'	S15:53.8'
21	131:30.3'	S15:53.0'

As you can see from the table, the sun crossed the Greenwich Meridian between 12:00 and 13:00. GHA increased to 359:59.9 then on crossing became 000:00.O.

UT (GMT)	GHA	DEC
20:00	116:30.3'	S15:53.8'
00:18:00	004:30.0'	-00:00.3'
————	————	————
20:18:00	121:00.3'	S15:53.5'

The ARC DISTANCE GHA 004:30.0' value came from the INCREMENTS and CORRECTIONS table that provides a between the hour GHA reading for each minute and second.

Between 20:00 and 21:00, DEC was reduced by 00:00.8 seconds. 18 minutes is approximately one third of a minute, therefore one third of 00:00.8' is approximately = 00:00.3'.

The results show that our position is:

Latitude:

90:00.0 =	89:60.0	53:53.3
Ho	-36:06.7	-15:53.5 (from almanac)
	————	————
	53:53.3	38:00N (during subtraction, I omitted the offsetting tenths) (When determining position, tenths are not used)

Longitude:

GHA = 121:00.3 therefore Longitude = 121:00 W-------WRONG, should be near 123:00 W (read on).

Background: My goal was to perform a noon sight plus two readings approximately 2 hours before and after the noon sight for a fix, all on the same day. All of the readings were fuzzy except the final one. On that, I discovered that by rotating the polarizing filter to the stop, the sun would kiss a flat black horizon. The final reading was easy and perfect. Rather than repeat the exercise on another day, I could use the fuzzy readings to simulate conditions in a seaway.

Secondly, with the fuzzy readings, I was forced to do a plot. While the latitude was steady and easy to interpret, the time of the meridian crossing was not. Using the plot, I picked 12:18 for the meridian crossing. Had I picked the crossing to be 12:19 or 12:20, the latitude would be unchanged but the longitude would have extended to the west.

The sun rotates 15 degrees/hour or 1 degree in four minutes or ¼ degree in one minute. At the equator this would be ¼ of 60nm or 15nm. At my latitude, 15nm is reduced by the cos of 38 degrees, which is .788 x 15nm or 11.8 2nm. If I had chosen the crossing at 12:19, the difference would have decreased by 12nm.

A re-examination of the longitude showed that it was off by almost 2 full degrees. My original interpretation of the meridian crossing computed a result of 121:00 W. The actual longitude is 122:52. After some severe head scratching, I took the midpoint of 2 identical altitude readings (denoted by asterisks) spaced 23 minutes apart. One was with the sun rising, the other with the sun falling. This resulted in a much more credible figure of 122:15 W.

The lesson here is to check the midpoint of the 2 farthest identical readings, especially when the sun is in the far hemisphere (FIG.06) (FIG. 07). A second lesson is to not expect accurate determination of longitude except when the sun is in your hemisphere. Note that the latitude should always be close.

GREAT CIRCLES

Great circles have a radius that CONNECTS the CENTER of the EARTH with both the NORTH and SOUTH POLES.

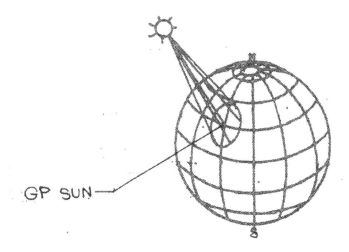

If the SUN is NOT on your MERIDIAN, it is NOT on your GREAT CIRCLE and any sight will generate a CIRCLE of EQUAL ALTITUDES. EQUAL ALTITUDES = EQUAL ANGLES = EQUAL HEIGHTS.

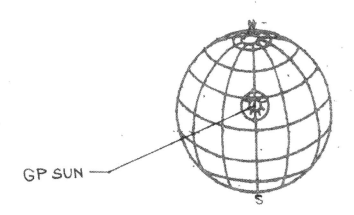

If the SUN is on your MERIDIAN, it is on a GREAT CIRCLE. This SPECIAL CIRCUMSTANCE has only TWO SOLUTIONS, the GP nearest the OBSERVER and a GP with an identical angle on the FAR SIDE of the MERIDIAN.

FIG. 04

LAT.	COS.		LATITUDE LENGTH	LONGITUDE LENGTH
90	0.000		POLE	ZERO
89	0.017	X	60	1.0
88	0.035	X	60	2.1
87	0.052	X	60	3.1
86	0.070	X	60	4.2
80	0.174	X	60	10.4
70	0.342	X	60	20.5
60	0.500	X	60	30
50	0.643	X	60	38.5
40	0.766	X	60	46
30	0.866	X	60	52
20	0.940	X	60	56.4
10	0.985	X	60	59.1
04	0.998	X	60	59.9
03	0.999	X	60	59.9
02	0.999	X	60	59.9
01	1.000	X	60	60
00	EQUATOR			60 nm

THIS TABLE REPRESENTS DECREASING
LONGITUDE WITH INCREASING LATITUDE

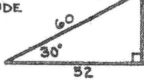

FIG. 05

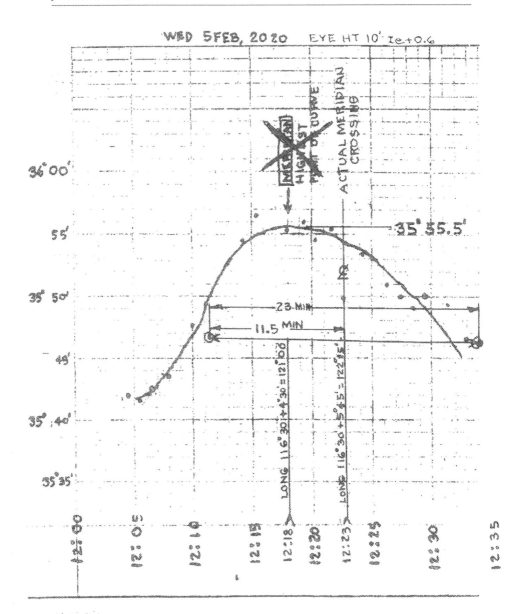

FIG. 06

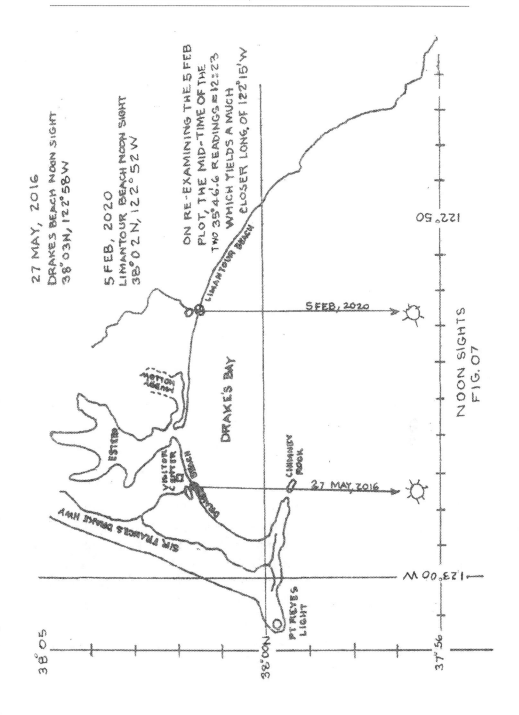

27 MAY, 2016
DRAKES BEACH NOON SIGHT
38°03N, 122°58W

5 FEB, 2020
LIMANTOUR BEACH NOON SIGHT
38°02 N, 122° 52 W

ON RE-EXAMINING THE 5 FEB
PLOT, THE MID-TIME OF THE
TWO 35°46.6 READINGS = 12:23
WHICH YIELDS A MUCH
CLOSER LONG, OF 122°15'W

LIMANTOUR BEACH

5 FEB, 2020

DRAKE'S BAY

ESTERO

LIMITOUR
SPITR
BEACH

CHIMNEY ROCK

27 MAY, 2016

SIR FRANCIS DRAKE HWY

PT REYES
LIGHT

38°05

38°00N

37° 56

123°00 W

122°50

NOON SIGHTS
FIG. 07

CHAPTER 6

CELESTIAL NAVAGATION WITH
AIR ALMANAC, HO 249

DEFINITIONS:

GP (Geographical Position):

A line between the CENTER of ANY heavenly body and the CENTER of the EARTH passes through its GP (Geographical Position), at the SURFACE. This single point GP on the surface of the earth is constantly moving. Think of it as a sharp instrument cutting threads on the surface. During a period of one year, the GP threads its way up to 23.5 degrees north, hangs there for a short time, (3 hours, according to the almanac), then begins threading its way south, across the equator and on to 23.5 degrees south. After hanging there for a short time, it threads its way north, crossing the equator to complete the cycle. This threading is the result of the spin of the earth and the elliptical path of its orbit around the sun. The ALMANAC locates the GP by DECLINATION, (DEC) (Latitude) and by GRENWICH HOUR ANGLE (GHA) (Longitude).

STOP, do not read further until you fully understand the information above. The GP is the KEY to navigation, your position is referenced to it. After this description is indelibly burned into your brain, you may continue.

DECLINATION:

The DECLINATION of a heavenly body is the LATITUDE of its GP.
DECLINATION = LATITUDE /// LATITUDE = DECLINATION.
The average rate of change is one degree every four days, 23.5 degrees every
91 days. It is listed in the almanac as (DEC).

HOUR ANGLE:

The HOUR ANGLE defines the LONGITUDE of the GP. The GHA is
the GREENWICH HOUR ANGLE. It is measured from the Greenwich
Meridian (longitude 000) in a westerly direction to GP. It is listed in the
almanac as (GHA). It is measured in ARC DEGREES, MINUTES, and
SECONDS.

If you are measuring the HOUR ANGLE from where you are standing,
this is defined as LHA. The LOCAL HOUR ANGLE is the distance in
degrees of longitude between the CELESTIAL OBJECT and YOU, the
observer. The LHA is always measured in a westerly direction (FIG.08).

TIME / ROTATION:

In 24-hours the earth rotates through 360 degrees of longitude. This
amounts to 15 degrees / hour (24 x 15 = 360). AT THE EQUATOR, the
distance is 1 degree (60 nm) / 4 minutes; 15 nm / minute; 1 nm/ 4 sec,
ALL ABOVE DISTANCES, ONLY AT THE EQUATOR.

Because the distance in miles between longitudinal meridians is
foreshortened by the multiplier of the (cosine x the latitude) as one moves
toward either pole, we will restrict our discussion to DEGREES OF
LONGITUDE rather than miles. Degrees are constant, distance varies.

As the earth slowly rotates from west to east, the observer watches the
sun rise in the east, slowly climb to its highest point in the sky at noon
on his MERIDIAN (LOCAL APPARENT NOON), then slowly start
descending until sunset in the west. Time can be equated to the angle
which the earth rotates through in a given period. In other words, TIME
can be equated to the ARC DISTANCE in longitude between two points.

TIME ZONES:

Time zones are 15 degrees wide. They are located between meridians of longitude. Zone 0 straddles the Greenwich meridian, 7 1/2 degrees East & West. Zone 8, straddles 120W, bordered between 112: 30 W & 127:30 W. Zone 12 extends to 180 EW, which marks the INTERNATIONAL DATE LINE. It is only 7 ½ degrees wide. Continuing west around earth, zone -12 lies between 180EW & 172:30E.

If the sun was on the GREENWICH MERIDIAN (000) at noon, 5 hours later it would be noon in New York (075 W), 6 hours later, noon Chicago (090 W), 8 hours later, noon San Francisco (120 W), 10 hours later, Honolulu (150 W). Refer to (FIG. 09).

FIX:

As mentioned earlier, on 05 FEB, 2020, I measured the sun approximately 2 hours before the noon sight and 3 hours after the noon sight in order to obtain a fix.

TIME	ANGLE		TIME	ANGLE
10:44:28	= 30:56.2		15:40:31	= 19:12.3
Hs	30:56.2		Hs	19:12.3
Ac	+ 14.9		Ac	+14.9
Ie +0.6	- 0.6		Ie +3.4	-3.4
DIP 10'	-3.1		DIP 12'	-3.4
	———			———
Ho	30:67.4 = 31:07.4		Ho	19:20.4

From ALMANAC, adding 8 hours for zone 8:

MORNING SUN SIGHT			AFTERNOON SUN SIGHT		
UT	GHA	DEC	UT	GHA	DEC
18:00	086:30.4	S15:55.3	23:00	161:30.2	S15:51.5
19:00	101:30.4	S15:54.5	00:00	176:30.1	S15:50.7
	———			———	
	-0.8			- 0.8	

18:00	086:30.4	S15:55.3	23:00	161:30.2	S15:51.5
00:44:24	11:06.0	-0.6	00:40:31	10:07.8	- 0.5
18:44:24	097:36.4	S15:54.7	23:40:31	171:38.0	S15:51.0

44 / 60 x 0.8 = 0.6 (DEC adjust)   40 / 60 x 0.8 = 0.5 (DEC adjust)

For a description of above, refer to work sheet, plot and tables, (FIG 11,12,13,14 & 22).

From table, GHA advanced 11:06.0 ARC DEGREES in 44min, 24sec (left column).

From table, GHA advanced 10:07.8 ARC DEGREES in 40min, 31sec (right column).

I interpolated the DEC to decrease ¾ x 0.8 min = 0.6 min (left column).

I interpolated the DEC to decrease 2/3 x 0.8min = 0.5 min (right column).

OVERVIEW:

HO 249, the AIR ALMANAC, contains solutions to the NAVIGATIONAL TRIANGLE for LATITUDES plus or minus 40 degrees NORTH or SOUTH of the EQUATOR and for CELESTIAL OBJECTS with DECLINATIONS up to 29 degrees above the horizon.

To select the proper page of HO 249, you must know the following:

1. Your LATITUDE.
2. The DEC of the celestial object. There is a range of 2 choice on adjacent pages, DEC (0-14) or (15-29) degrees.
3. Whether the object is in your hemisphere, SAME NAME, or not, CONTRARY NAME.
4. The LHA, Local Hour Angle.

On the correct page, find the intersection of the LHA and DEC in the table.

We will come out of the table with three pieces of data, (Hc, d, Z) which will be discussed after they have been determined.

LHA: Local Hour Angle is the distance measured westerly, between our position and the GP of the sun or other heavenly body. We must enter the table with an even LHA, no minutes, no seconds.

In the first example, (morning sight), the GHA (longitude) of the sun is 97:36.4. We must ASSUME a LONGITUDE in order to determine our distance to the GHA of the sun. I know that I am near 123:00 W, the dead reckoning, DR longitude position. I make the Assumed Long (AP), 122:36.4 so that when I subtract it from the sun's GHA (- if west) it will be an even number. Because my AP must be subtracted from GHA, I must add 360 which becomes 457:36.4. The LHA result now becomes an even 335 degrees.

In the second example, the GHA of the sun is 171:38.0. I make the Assumed Long 122:38.0, the difference in this case is 49. LHA = 49.

NAVAGATION TRIANGLE:

Before entering the HO 249 tables, it is imperative to understand what is going on. The navigation triangle has 3 corners, the north or south pole, the GP of the celestial body, and our position (FIG.10). HO 249 contains the solutions to all of the possible triangles between the equator and 40 degrees north or south. Volume 3 of HO 249 contains solutions for higher latitudes.

To use the tables, we must be aware of which hemisphere we are in, the hemisphere of the GP and our approximate position, ASSUMED POSITION. We tell the tables where we think we are, the table solution, (argument) then tells us where we actually are. The table provides a LINE OF POSITION as the solution for each individual sight. This is revealed as an AZIMUTH (Z), a calculated height angle (Hc), and a (d) correction which must be processed in TABLE 5.

We enter the tables by locating the correct page. The page we are looking for contains our LATITUDE, the DECLINATION of the heavenly body in question, and whether or not the GP is in our hemisphere (SAME NAME / CONTRARY NAME). We find the solution at the intersection of LHA and DEC.

HO 249 TABLE:

The correct table with the solutions that will provide a FIX for our sights is listed below. Both solutions are on the same page. To use the table, we find the solutions at the intersections of the DECLINATION column of 15 degrees and the row of LHA 334 and the row of LHA 48.

LAT 38 degrees [DECLINATION (15-29 degrees) CONTRARY NAME TO LATITUDE]

	15 degrees				15 degrees		
	Hc	d	Z		Hc	d	Z
LHA 335	33:02	-56	151	LHA 49	19:53	-47	129

To make use of these two solutions, the results must be transferred to the appropriate work sheet.

Hc is the calculated sight angle (HEIGHT) and defines where we are on the great circle.

(d) is a correction that when combined with the DECLINATION minutes in TABLE 5, the result will be added to or subtracted from Hc.

(Z) is an azimuth which points to the GP of our sight. At the upper left-hand corner and lower left-hand corner of our table are notes describing how to convert Z to Zn so we can complete our plot. We choose the directions in the upper left corner with a bracket marked (N. Lat) because we are located in the NORTHERN HEMISPHERE. If we were south of the equator, the notes in the lower left corner would apply.

LHA greater then 180 degrees.....Zn = Z
LHA less than 180 degrees...........Zn = 360 − Z

By applying the above instructions to the applicable LHAs we convert Z to Zn.

For LHA 335, Zn = 151 degrees
For LHA 49, Zn = (360 − 129) = 231 degrees

TABLE 5:

The table above only allows entry for an even DECLINATION. The remainder is rounded off and entered into TABLE 5 where it is averaged with the calculated (d). TABLE 5 is set up with rows and columns. The RESULT is the same whether the first entry is made in a row or column. Depending on the sign, the RESULT is added to or subtracted from Hc.

FINAL RESULT:

Ho and Hc are compared based on metaphors: HOMOTO the fictional Japanese navigator or COAST GUARD ACADAMY. Ho more TOWARDS, Hc greater AWAY. Hc is the calculated height of the angle that determines our location on the CIRCLE OF EQUAL ALTITUDES. The observed height Ho is compared to Hc. If Ho is greater, the location of the CIRCLE OF EQUAL ALTITUDES is moved (T) towards the GP for the plot on azimuth line Zn and the distance is listed as (T). If it compares less, the difference is listed away (A) and plotted accordingly. The result is a LINE OF POSITION (LOP).

The FIX is determined by the intersection of two or more CIRCLES OF EQUAL ALTITUDE. The circles are so large that they can be represented on the plot by straight lines. Once again, each plot is done with the Zn (azimuth) and the distance (T) toward or (A) away from the CELESTIAL OBJECT.

The reader can readily see the advantage of the NOON SIGHT. It provides a numerical position in a short period of time, with a precise latitude and a reasonably close longitude. This, without the four or five-hour spacing, computations, HO 249 book lookup, and the plot sheet.

An accurate FIX can also be done by use of the 57 NAVIGATIONAL STARS, planets VENUS, MARS, SATURN, and JUPITOR or the MOON.

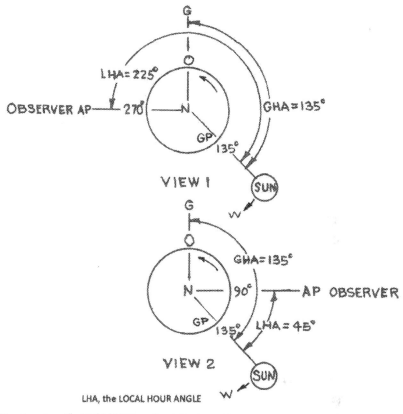

LHA, the LOCAL HOUR ANGLE

Looking down from the NORTH POLE, earth rotation is west to east.

Fron observer position, the SUN and other CELESTIAL OBJECTS move from EAST to WEST.

Let "G" indicate the GREENWICH MERIDIAN, 000.00.

Let "GHA" indicate the GREENWICH HOUR ANGLE (longitude distance).

Let "LHA" (LOCAL HOUR ANGLE) indicate our distance to GHA, always measured WESTWARD from GHA.

Let "AP" indicate our position (assumed position) (observer)

Let "SUN" indicate the sun's position.

VIEW 1

The OBVERSER is to the WEST of the SUN. LHA is always measured in a WESTWARD direction, therefore to determine LHA, you must ADD (360-270), 90 degrees + 135 degrees. LHA = 225 degrees.

View 2

The OBSERVER is to the EAST of the SUN. LHA is simply the difference of the two positions. LHA is 135 – 90 degrees, therefore LHA = 45 degrees. FIG. O8

41

TIME / ROTATION

	LAT.	ZONE	RANGE
DATE LINE	180	-12	172½ E TO 180
	165E	-11	157½ E TO 172½ E
	150E	-10	142½ E TO 157½ E
	135E	-9	127½ E TO 142½ E
	120 E	-8	112½ E TO 127½ E
	105E	-7	97½ E TO 112½ E
	90E	-6	82½ E TO 97½ E
	75E	-5	67½ E TO 82½ E
	60E	-4	52½ E TO 67½ E
	45E	-3	37½ E TO 52½ E
	30E	-2	22½ E TO 37½ E
	15E	-1	7½ E TO 22½ E
GREENWICH	000	0	7½ W TO 7½ E
	15W	1	7½ W TO 22½ W
	30W	2	22½ W TO 37½ W
	45W	3	37½ W TO 52½ W
	60W	4	52½ W TO 67½ W
NEW YORK	75W	5	67½ W TO 82½ W
	90W	6	82½ W TO 97½ W
	105W	7	97½ W TO 112½ W
SAN FRANCISCO	120W	8	112½ W TO 127½ W
	135W	9	127½ W TO 142½ W
HONOLULU	150W	10	142½ W TO 157½ W
	165W	11	157½ W TO 172½ W
DATE LINE	180	12	172½ W TO 180

TIME ZONES

FIG.09

THE NAVAGATIONAL TRIANGLE

The NAVAGATIONAL TRIANGLE consists of 3 points, the NORTH or SOUTH POLE, the GP of a heavenly body and our AP (assumed position).

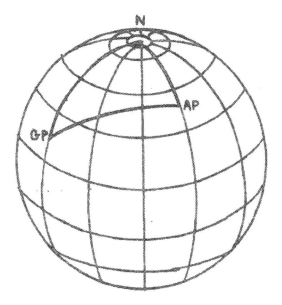

STEP 1. In order to find our location, we must reference our position to the GP of a heavenly body. We take a sight (Ha) on the body at a specific time. After some adjustments we determine Ho.

STEP 2. We must now determine the position, GP of our reference body. The lat/lon, DEC and GHA are determined from the NAUTICAL ALMANAC.

STEP 3. With the GP position established, we determine our distance (LHA) to the body and its declination, (DEC). We decide whether the body is in our hemisphere, (SAME NAME, or not, CONTRARY NAME) With these 3 bits of information, + OUR (LAT), we enter HO249 on the correct page.

STEP 4. HO249 provides the solution to the NAVAGATIONAL TRIANGLE. It provides us with 3 bits of information, calculated altitude (Hc), azimuth (Z) and a correction (v) to be used in TABLE 5.

STEP 5. With the result from the 2 inputs to TABLE 5 and a few more adjustments, we end with an azimuth (Zn) and a distance toward or away from a great circle. This is our LINE OF POSITION which we can plot. If we have 2 or more LOPs we will have a FIX, our position, where the lines cross. (INTERCEPT).

FIG. 10

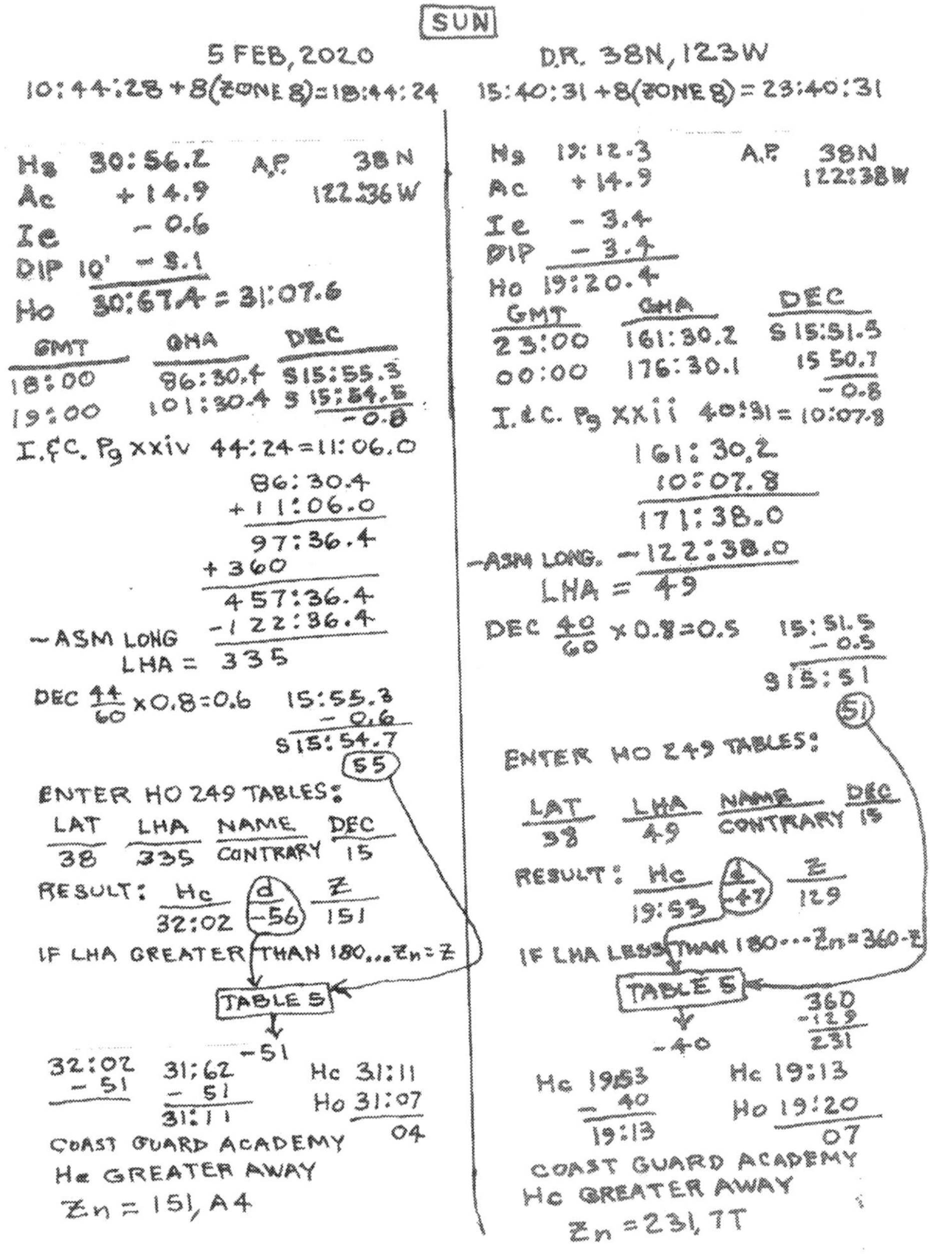

$\boxed{\text{SUN}}$

5 FEB, 2020   D.R. 38N, 123W

10:44:28 +8(ZONE 8)=18:44:24   15:40:31 +8(ZONE 8) = 23:40:31

Hs	30:56.2	A.P. 38N
Ac	+ 14.9	122:36 W
Ie	− 0.6	
DIP 10'	− 3.1	
Ho	30:67.4 = 31:07.6	

GMT	GHA	DEC
18:00	86:30.4	S15:55.3
19:00	101:30.4	S 15:54.5
		−0.8

I.fC. Pg xxiv 44:24=11:06.0

```
    86:30.4
  +11:06.0
   97:36.4
    +360
  457:36.4
 -122:36.4
LHA = 335
```

~ASM LONG

DEC $\frac{44}{60}$ ×0.8=0.6   15:55.3
             −0.6
             S15:54.7 (55)

ENTER HO 249 TABLES:

LAT	LHA	NAME	DEC
38	335	CONTRARY	15

RESULT: Hc   d   Z
        32:02   (−56)   151

IF LHA GREATER THAN 180...Zn=Z

$\boxed{\text{TABLE 5}}$

          −51
32:02   31:62   Hc 31:11
− 51   − 51   Ho 31:07
       31:11   04

COAST GUARD ACADEMY
Hc GREATER AWAY
Zn = 151, A4

Hs	19:12.3	A.P. 38N
Ac	+ 14.9	122:38 W
Ie	− 3.4	
DIP	− 3.4	
Ho	19:20.4	

GMT	GHA	DEC
23:00	161:30.2	S15:51.3
00:00	176:30.1	15 50.7
		−0.8

I.&C. Pg XXii 40:31 = 10:07.8

```
   161:30.2
    10:07.8
   171:38.0
-122:38.0
LHA = 49
```

−ASM LONG.

DEC $\frac{40}{60}$ × 0.8=0.5   15:51.5
                −0.5
             S15:51 (51)

ENTER HO 249 TABLES:

LAT	LHA	NAME	DEC
38	49	CONTRARY	15

RESULT: Hc   d   Z
       19:53   (−47)   129

IF LHA LESS THAN 180...Zn=360-Z

$\boxed{\text{TABLE 5}}$

          360
     −40   −129
              231

Hc 19:53   Hc 19:13
   − 40   Ho 19:20
   19:13   07

COAST GUARD ACADEMY
Hc GREATER AWAY
Zn = 231, 7T

FIG. 11

FROM NAUTICAL ALMANAC

2020 FEBRUARY 3, 4, 5 (MON., TUES., WED.) 33

The inset (zoomed) SUN table:

UT	SUN	
	GHA	Dec
d h	° ′	° ′
3 00	176 34.5	S16 44.3
01	191 34.4	43.6
02	206 34.3	42.9
03	221 34.3 ..	42.2
04	236 34.2	41.4
05	251 34.1	40.7
20	116 31.6	...
21	131 31.5 ..	11.1
22	146 31.5	10.4
23	161 31.4	09.6
5 00	176 31.4	S16 08.9
01	191 31.3	08.1
02	206 31.3	07.4
03	221 31.2 ..	06.6
04	236 31.1	05.9
05	251 31.1	05.1
06	266 31.0	S16 04.4
07	281 31.0	03.6
08	296 30.9	02.9
09	311 30.9 ..	02.1
10	326 30.8	01.4
11	341 30.8	16 00.6
12	356 30.7	S15 59.8
13	11 30.7	59.1
14	26 30.6	58.3
15	41 30.6 ..	57.6
16	56 30.5	56.8
17	71 30.5	56.1
18	86 30.4	S15 55.3
19	101 30.4	54.5
20	116 30.3	53.8
21	131 30.3 ..	53.0
22	146 30.2	52.3
23	161 30.2	51.5
	SD 16.3	d 0.7	SD

FOR SUN SIGHTS, 5 FEB, 2020
FIG. 12

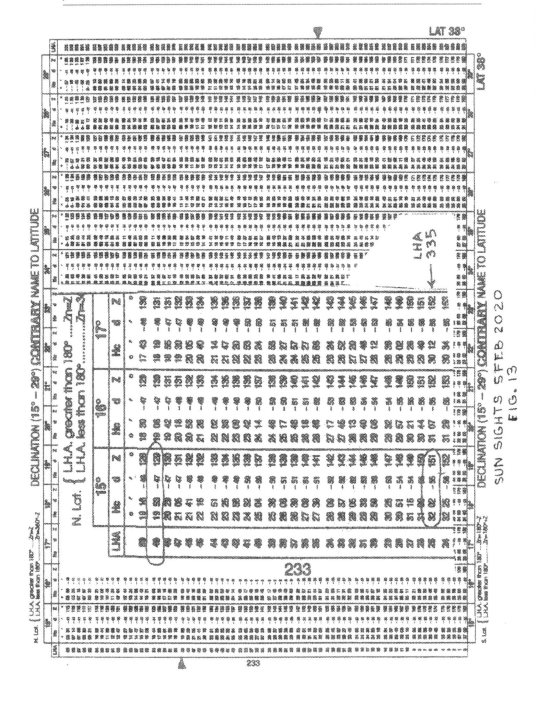

SUN SIGHTS 5 FEB 2020
FIG. 13

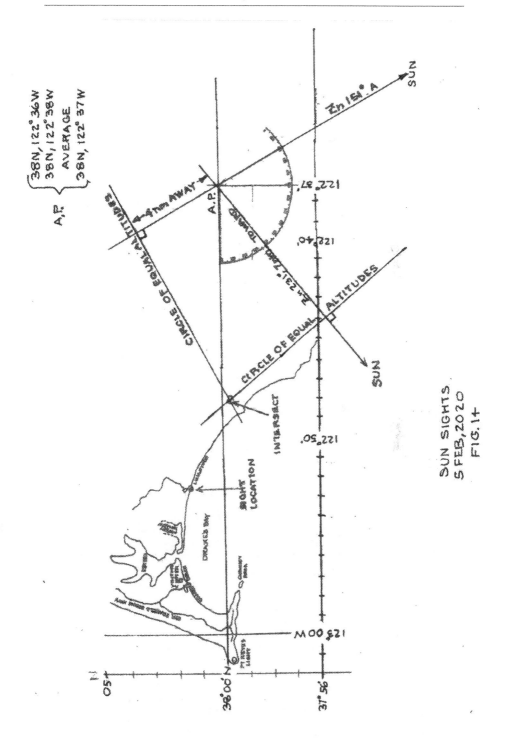

SUN SIGHTS
5 FEB, 2020
FIG. 14

CHAPTER 7

RECONSTRUCTED SIGHT, VENUS & SIRIUS

In the early morning of 15 OCT, 2020, I measured the altitudes of VENUS and SIRIUS, two of the brightest and easiest objects to identify. Unfortunately, the horizon was somewhat obscured by a marine layer. It can be difficult and frustrating, taking sights on the coast. After some difficult consideration, I tossed my notes.

While writing this manuscript, I decided that it would be possible to reconstruct the measurements, working backward from the FIX. I had the advantage, the data was taken from my favorite location on the shore of LIMANTOUR beach, it was the morning twilight, and my plot sheet contained a protractor and the LAT/LON labels. In the process the adjustments and corrections of the sight would be systematically revealed. Facing due south, with the image of the protractor burned into my brain, VENUS was on my left (east), and SIRIUS was directly south.

I had first measured SIRIUS and was waiting for VENUS to move south to clear the beach to provide a horizon. At the same time the SUN was rising. The range of opportunity for taking morning and evening sights is approximately ten minutes. There exists a fine balance. The observer must be able to find and resolve the celestial image and the backlight must provide a horizon.

Venus is different from a star. It is one of the brightest objects in the sky and is usually visible until sunrise. It was a race to move its GP west to clear the beach, providing a horizon before being extinguished from the sunrise. It barely made it before disappearing. On reaching the horizon, over water, the Zn (true azimuth, measured from my plot sheet) was 129 degrees.

Thinking back, I decided to reconstruct the sights from the ALMANAC and HO 249. The planet VENUS, and the star, SIRIUS, are two of the brightest and easiest objects to locate in the dark sky. This exercise should prove helpful in understanding the process and the HO 249 tables.

INITIAL SETUP: 15 OCT,2020, DR position 38:00 N, 123:00 W

SIRIUS

We will begin with SIRIUS, due south with a fuzzy horizon, early in the morning during NAUTICAL TWILIGHT. In order to establish the time of the reconstructed sight, we must refer to the sunrise-twilight table, FIG. 15, (righthand page [203] for OCTOBER 15, 16, 17),

The table is set up with latitude (Lat. on the left column, Twilight, Naut, and Civil in the center, and Sunrise to the right). The page lists info for 3 days. The morning Naut Twilight represents the middle day, in this case the 16th.

To use the table (upper one with SUNRISE), we scroll down to the nearest latitude, N 40, the closest to 38. The two times of concern are NAUTICAL TWIILIGHT, 05:13 and SUNRISE, 06:12, when the SUN will blank VENUS. The usual viewing time when the celestial object is visible in the sextant and the horizon can be used is about ten minutes. Sirius, one of the brightest objects in the sky can be seen for over 20 minutes.

Let us pick 05:32:00 for the SIRIUS sight, this is a reconstruction (ref. FIG. 16, 17, 20).

If we were in Greenwich, we could begin at 05:32:00. For zone 8, we add 8 hours = 13:32:00.

The GHA of a star (SIRIUS) is the SUM of the GHA of ARIES and the SHA of the star.

All stars are referenced from ARIES, the first point of ARIES the RAM, the first moment of the south to north crossing of the equator, the (VERNAL EQUINOX).

All stars are grouped together by their relative position to one another. This position label is termed the SHA, SIDERIAL HOUR ANGLE.

At UT (GMT) 13:00, GHA, AIRES = 219:31.1. (FIG. 16)

From "Increments and corrections", pg xviii, 32 min= 8:01.3

The GHA ARIES at UT (GMT)13:32 = 219:31.1 + 8:01.3 = 227:32.4

From STARS, FIG 16, Sirius

	SHA	DEC
	258:29.2	S16:44.5

GHA SIRIUS = 258:29.2 + GHA ARIES, 227:32.4 = 485:61.6= 486:01.6.

This is where you create the ASSUMED LONGITUDE POSITION. Our DR longitude is 123:00 W. We must create an ASM LONG. That when subtracted from the celestial GHA yields a whole number termed LHA, the LOCAL HOUR ANGLE We pick 123:01.6, a contrived number near the DR POSITION.

GHA SIRIUS, 486:01.6 – 123:01.6 = LHA, 363.

There can only be 360 degrees in a circle, therefor LHA = 363 – 360. (LHA=3).

SIRIUS resides in the SOUTHERN HEMISPHERE at DEC, S16:44.5. We are in the northern hemisphere at 38N. Because SIRIUS is not in our hemisphere, we enter HO249 as NAME – CONTRARY.

We now can enter the HO 249 TABLES. (FIG. 17): LAT 38 / LHA 3 / NAME - CONTRARY / Dec. 16.

TABLE result:	Hc	d	Z
	35:56	-60	176

In the upper left corner of the TABLE, a note states that: If the LHA < 180....Zn = 360 – Z

Use the UPPER corner notes if you are in the NORTHERN HEMISPHERE.

Use the LOWER corner notes if you are located in the SOUTHERN HEMISPHERE.

Zn = 360 -176. Zn =184

TABLE 5 (FIG. 14) is used to resolve the (d correction) of the celestial object minutes.

The minutes of SIRIUS DEC, 16: 44.5 must be rounded and combined with the – 60 d correction inside TABLE 5. The result (- 45) is then added to or subtracted from Hc.

Note: TABLE 5 yields the same results whether (d) is entered from the top or the side.

The result of TABLE 5 with inputs (d /-60) and SIRIUS DEC minutes, 45 = -45.

Hc = 35:56 – 45 = 35:11. I have arbitrarily picked Ho to be 35:14 to make the plot simple. By using the "COAST GUARD ACADEMY" rule, (if Hc GREATER, AWAY) to remember whether to add to or subtract Ho from Hc,. In our case, with Hc less than Ho, the difference yields 3 nautical miles (T) towards SIRIUS with an azimuth of Zn = 184.

VENUS

The VENUS "sight" was taken 15 OCT. 2020. We know the answer to the where are we question. The spot on Limantour beach is marked with a protractor. We will now reconstruct the sight.

As we begin the regression process, the sun is rising and moving west, but is not yet over the water for a horizon. The Zn (azimuth) must reach 129 before the sun blanks out Venus. We assume a time of 06:00 for the first sight, sunrise is 06:12 (FIG. 15). Data for Venus is listed on the left-hand page of the ALMANAC (FIG.16).

				06:00
UT(GMT)	GHA	DEC.	+ ZONE 8	8
14:00	067:58.0	N6:52.6		14:00
ADD 360	360			
	427:58.0			
	-122:58.0	SUBTRACT ASM. POS. FOR LHA		
LHA =	305			

WE CAN NOW ENTER THE HO 249 TABLES (FIG. 18):

LAT	LHA	NAME	DEC.	RESULT:	Hc	d	Z
38	305	SAME	N6		30:55	40	108

IF LHA GREATER THAN 180.....Zn = Z   Zn = 108

OUR REQUIREMENT IS FOR Zn = 129. WE SCAN THE TABLE FOR Z = 129:

LAT	LHA	NAME	DEC.	RESULT:	Hc	d	Z
38	327	SAME	N6		46:11	47	129

LHA = 327   Z = 129

IF LHA GREATER THAN 180....Zn = Z   Zn = 129

Coast Guard Academy, (Hc greater away)

We select an Ho that simplifies the plot: Ho   46:13

                                                   46:11

                                                   02

FFROM OUR KNOWN POSITION: Zn = 129, T2

I must confess that this used to be a difficult subject for me. I write as a person who stumbled and became lost while following exercises in "HOW TO" books, written by expert navigational instructors. I would be following the calculations and suddenly wonder what was going on and where was I? It is imperative to be cognizant of where you are in the process and to understand the definitions. My drawings and text are an attempt to simplify and clarify this process.

It is my hope that the preceding exercises have revealed the basic celestial navigation process in a clear and easy to understand way. My primary goal is for the reader to understand the principles. All this becomes much easier with repetition. Now you should be prepared to tackle the books written by the experts. Happy navigation!

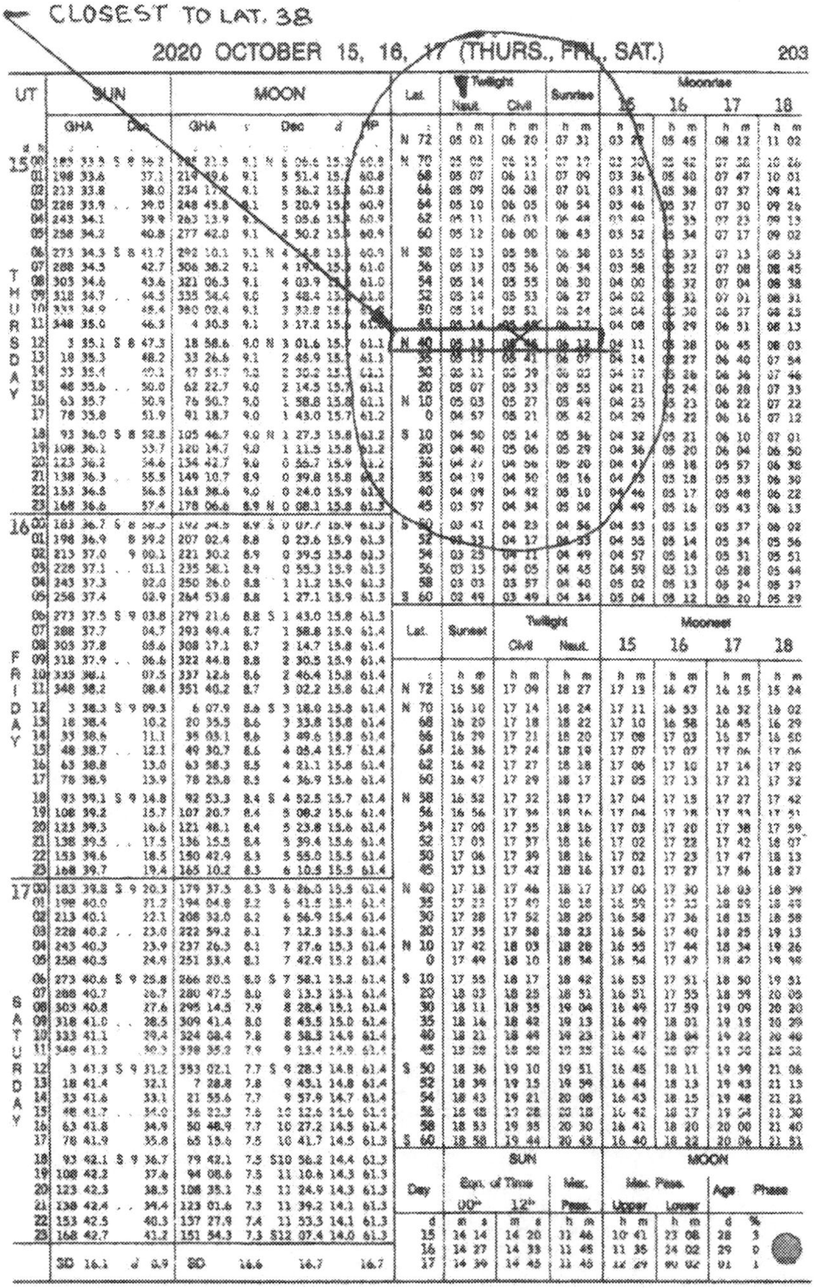
CLOSEST TO LAT. 38

2020 OCTOBER 15, 16, 17 (THURS., FRI., SAT.) 203

UT	SUN GHA	SUN Dec	MOON GHA	v	MOON Dec	d	HP
d h	° ′	° ′	° ′	′	° ′	′	′
15 00	183 33.5	S 8 36.2	[illegible] 21.8	9.1	N 6 06.6	15.2	60.8
01	198 33.6	37.1	219 49.6	9.1	5 51.4	15.[illegible]	60.8
02	213 33.8	38.0	234 17.7	9.1	5 36.2	15.3	60.8
03	228 33.9	39.0	248 45.8	9.1	5 20.9	15.3	60.9
04	243 34.1	39.9	263 13.9	9.1	5 05.6	15.4	60.9
05	258 34.2	40.8	277 42.0	9.1	4 50.2	15.4	60.9
06	273 34.3	S 8 41.7	292 10.1	9.1	N 4 34.8	15.[illegible]	60.9
07	288 34.5	42.7	306 38.2	9.1	4 19.[illegible]	15.[illegible]	61.0
08	303 34.6	43.6	321 06.3	9.1	4 03.9	[illegible]	61.0
09	318 34.7	44.5	335 34.4	9.0	3 48.4	15.[illegible]	61.0
10	333 34.9	45.4	350 02.4	9.1	3 32.8	15.[illegible]	[illegible]
11	348 35.0	46.3	4 30.5	9.1	3 17.2	15.[illegible]	61.[illegible]
12	3 35.1	S 8 47.3	18 58.6	9.0	N 3 01.6	15.7	61.1
13	18 35.3	48.2	33 26.6	9.1	2 45.9	15.7	61.1
14	33 35.4	49.1	47 54.7	9.0	2 30.2	15.7	61.1
15	48 35.6	50.0	62 22.7	9.0	2 14.5	15.7	61.1
16	63 35.7	50.9	76 50.7	9.0	1 58.8	15.8	61.1
17	78 35.8	51.9	91 18.7	9.0	1 43.0	15.7	61.2
18	93 36.0	S 8 52.8	105 46.7	9.0	N 1 27.3	15.8	61.2
19	108 36.1	53.7	120 14.7	9.0	1 11.5	15.8	61.2
20	123 36.2	54.6	134 42.7	9.0	0 55.7	15.9	61.2
21	138 36.3	55.5	149 10.7	8.9	0 39.8	15.8	61.2
22	153 36.5	56.5	163 38.6	9.0	0 24.0	15.9	61.3
23	168 36.6	57.4	178 06.6	8.9	N 0 08.1	15.8	61.3
16 00	183 36.7	S 8 58.3	192 34.5	8.9	S 0 07.7	15.9	61.3
01	198 36.9	8 59.2	207 02.4	8.8	0 23.6	15.9	61.3
02	213 37.0	9 00.1	221 30.2	8.9	0 39.5	15.8	61.3
03	228 37.1	01.1	235 58.1	8.9	0 55.3	15.9	61.3
04	243 37.3	02.0	250 26.0	8.8	1 11.2	15.9	61.3
05	258 37.4	02.9	264 53.8	8.8	1 27.1	15.9	61.3
06	273 37.5	S 9 03.8	279 21.6	8.8	S 1 43.0	15.8	61.3
07	288 37.7	04.7	293 49.4	8.7	1 58.8	15.9	61.4
08	303 37.8	05.6	308 17.1	8.7	2 14.7	15.8	61.4
09	318 37.9	06.6	322 44.8	8.8	2 30.5	15.9	61.4
10	333 38.1	07.5	337 12.6	8.6	2 46.4	15.8	61.4
11	348 38.2	08.4	351 40.2	8.7	3 02.2	15.8	61.4
12	3 38.3	S 9 09.3	6 07.9	8.6	S 3 18.0	15.8	61.4
13	18 38.4	10.2	20 35.5	8.6	3 33.8	15.8	61.4
14	33 38.6	11.1	35 03.1	8.6	3 49.6	15.8	61.4
15	48 38.7	12.1	49 30.7	8.6	4 05.4	15.7	61.4
16	63 38.8	13.0	63 58.3	8.5	4 21.1	15.8	61.4
17	78 38.9	13.9	78 25.8	8.5	4 36.9	15.6	61.4
18	93 39.1	S 9 14.8	92 53.3	8.4	S 4 52.5	15.7	61.4
19	108 39.2	15.7	107 20.7	8.4	5 08.2	15.6	61.4
20	123 39.3	16.6	121 48.1	8.4	5 23.8	15.6	61.4
21	138 39.5	17.5	136 15.5	8.4	5 39.4	15.6	61.4
22	153 39.6	18.5	150 42.9	8.3	5 55.0	15.5	61.4
23	168 39.7	19.4	165 10.2	8.3	6 10.5	15.5	61.4
17 00	183 39.8	S 9 20.3	179 37.5	8.3	S 6 26.0	15.5	61.4
01	198 40.0	21.2	194 04.8	8.2	6 41.5	15.4	61.4
02	213 40.1	22.1	208 32.0	8.2	6 56.9	15.4	61.4
03	228 40.2	23.0	222 59.2	8.1	7 12.3	15.3	61.4
04	243 40.3	23.9	237 26.3	8.1	7 27.6	15.3	61.4
05	258 40.5	24.9	251 53.4	8.1	7 42.9	15.2	61.4
06	273 40.6	S 9 25.8	266 20.5	8.0	S 7 58.1	15.2	61.4
07	288 40.7	26.7	280 47.5	8.0	8 13.3	15.1	61.4
08	303 40.8	27.6	295 14.5	7.9	8 28.4	15.1	61.4
09	318 41.0	28.5	309 41.4	8.0	8 43.5	15.0	61.4
10	333 41.1	29.4	324 08.4	7.8	8 58.5	14.9	61.4
11	348 41.2	30.3	338 35.2	7.9	9 13.4	14.9	61.4
12	3 41.3	S 9 31.2	353 02.1	7.7	S 9 28.3	14.8	61.4
13	18 41.4	32.1	7 28.8	7.8	9 43.1	14.8	61.4
14	33 41.6	33.1	21 55.6	7.7	9 57.9	14.7	61.4
15	48 41.7	34.0	36 22.3	7.6	10 12.6	14.6	61.4
16	63 41.8	34.9	50 48.9	7.7	10 27.2	14.5	61.4
17	78 41.9	35.8	65 15.6	7.5	10 41.7	14.5	61.3
18	93 42.1	S 9 36.7	79 42.1	7.5	S 10 56.2	14.4	61.3
19	108 42.2	37.6	94 08.6	7.5	11 10.6	14.3	61.3
20	123 42.3	38.5	108 35.1	7.5	11 24.9	14.3	61.3
21	138 42.4	39.4	123 01.6	7.3	11 39.2	14.1	61.3
22	153 42.5	40.3	137 27.9	7.4	11 53.3	14.1	61.3
23	168 42.7	41.2	151 54.3	7.3	S 12 07.4	14.0	61.3
	SD 16.1	d 0.9	SD 16.6		16.7		16.7

Lat.	Twilight Naut.	Twilight Civil	Sunrise	Moonrise 15	Moonrise 16	Moonrise 17	Moonrise 18
°	h m	h m	h m	h m	h m	h m	h m
N 72	05 01	06 20	07 31	03 2[illegible]	05 45	08 12	11 02
N 70	05 05	06 15	07 19	03 30	05 42	07 58	10 26
68	05 07	06 11	07 09	03 36	05 40	07 47	10 01
66	05 09	06 08	07 01	03 41	05 38	07 37	09 41
64	05 10	06 05	06 54	03 46	05 37	07 30	09 26
62	05 11	06 03	06 48	03 49	05 35	07 23	09 13
60	05 12	06 00	06 43	03 52	05 34	07 17	09 02
N 58	05 13	05 58	06 38	03 55	05 33	07 13	08 53
56	05 13	05 56	06 34	03 58	05 32	07 08	08 45
54	05 14	05 55	06 30	04 00	05 32	07 04	08 38
52	05 14	05 53	06 27	04 02	05 31	07 01	08 31
50	05 14	05 51	06 24	04 04	05 30	06 57	08 25
45	05 14	05 48	06 17	04 08	05 29	06 51	08 13
N 40	05 13	05 [illegible]	06 12	04 11	05 28	06 45	08 03
35	05 12	05 41	06 07	04 14	05 27	06 40	07 54
30	05 11	05 39	06 03	04 17	05 26	06 36	07 46
20	05 07	05 33	05 55	04 21	05 24	06 28	07 33
N 10	05 03	05 27	05 49	04 25	05 23	06 22	07 22
0	04 57	05 21	05 42	04 29	05 22	06 16	07 12
S 10	04 50	05 14	05 36	04 32	05 21	06 10	07 01
20	04 40	05 06	05 29	04 36	05 20	06 04	06 50
30	04 27	04 56	05 20	04 41	05 18	05 57	06 38
35	04 19	04 50	05 16	04 43	05 18	05 53	06 30
40	04 09	04 42	05 10	04 46	05 17	05 48	06 22
45	03 57	04 34	05 04	04 49	05 16	05 43	06 13
S 50	03 41	04 23	04 56	04 53	05 15	05 37	06 02
52	03 33	04 17	04 53	04 55	05 14	05 34	05 56
54	03 25	04 11	04 49	04 57	05 14	05 31	05 51
56	03 15	04 05	04 45	04 59	05 13	05 28	05 44
58	03 03	03 57	04 40	05 02	05 13	05 24	05 37
S 60	02 49	03 49	04 34	05 04	05 12	05 20	05 29

Lat.	Sunset	Twilight Civil	Twilight Naut.	Moonset 15	Moonset 16	Moonset 17	Moonset 18
°	h m	h m	h m	h m	h m	h m	h m
N 72	15 58	17 09	18 27	17 13	16 47	16 15	15 24
N 70	16 10	17 14	18 24	17 11	16 53	16 32	16 02
68	16 20	17 18	18 22	17 10	16 58	16 45	16 29
66	16 29	17 21	18 20	17 08	17 03	16 57	16 50
64	16 36	17 24	18 19	17 07	17 07	17 06	17 06
62	16 42	17 27	18 18	17 06	17 10	17 14	17 20
60	16 47	17 29	18 17	17 05	17 13	17 21	17 32
N 58	16 52	17 32	18 17	17 04	17 15	17 27	17 42
56	16 56	17 34	18 16	17 04	17 18	17 33	17 51
54	17 00	17 35	18 16	17 03	17 20	17 38	17 59
52	17 03	17 37	18 16	17 02	17 22	17 42	18 07
50	17 06	17 39	18 16	17 02	17 23	17 47	18 13
45	17 13	17 42	18 16	17 01	17 27	17 56	18 27
N 40	17 18	17 46	18 17	17 00	17 30	18 03	18 39
35	17 23	17 49	18 18	16 59	17 33	18 09	18 49
30	17 28	17 52	18 20	16 58	17 36	18 15	18 58
20	17 35	17 58	18 23	16 56	17 40	18 25	19 13
N 10	17 42	18 03	18 28	16 55	17 44	18 34	19 26
0	17 49	18 10	18 34	16 54	17 47	18 42	19 38
S 10	17 55	18 17	18 42	16 53	17 51	18 50	19 51
20	18 03	18 25	18 51	16 51	17 55	18 59	20 05
30	18 11	18 35	19 04	16 49	17 59	19 09	20 20
35	18 16	18 42	19 13	16 49	18 01	19 15	20 29
40	18 21	18 49	19 23	16 47	18 04	19 22	20 40
45	18 28	18 58	19 35	16 46	18 07	19 30	20 52
S 50	18 36	19 10	19 51	16 45	18 11	19 39	21 06
52	18 39	19 15	19 59	16 44	18 13	19 43	21 13
54	18 43	19 21	20 08	16 43	18 15	19 48	21 21
56	18 48	19 28	20 18	16 42	18 17	19 54	21 30
58	18 53	19 35	20 30	16 41	18 20	20 00	21 40
S 60	18 58	19 44	20 45	16 40	18 22	20 06	21 51

Day	SUN Eqn. of Time 00ʰ	SUN Eqn. of Time 12ʰ	SUN Mer. Pass.	MOON Mer. Pass. Upper	MOON Mer. Pass. Lower	MOON Age	MOON Phase
d	m s	m s	h m	h m	h m	d	%
15	14 14	14 20	11 46	10 41	23 08	28	3
16	14 27	14 33	11 45	11 35	24 02	29	0
17	14 39	14 45	11 45	12 29	00 02	01	1

NAUTICAL ALMANAC – SUNRISE DETAIL

FIG. 15

UT	ARIES GHA	VENUS −4.0 GHA	Dec	MARS −2.6 GHA	Dec	JUPITER −2.3 GHA	Dec	SATURN +0.5 GHA	Dec
d h									
15 00	23 59.0	218 02.9	N 7 07.2	3 42.5	N 5 23.1	93 20.2	S22 31.5	86 24.3	S21 21.0
01	39 01.5	233 02.5	06.2	18 45.3	23.0	108 22.4	31.4	101 26.7	21.0
02	54 03.9	248 02.2	05.2	33 49.0	22.9	123 24.6	31.4	116 29.1	21.0
03	69 06.4	263 01.8 ..	04.1	48 52.3	22.7	138 26.8 ..	31.4	131 31.5 ..	21.0
04	84 08.9	278 01.5	03.1	63 55.5	22.6	153 29.0	31.3	146 33.9	21.0
05	99 11.3	293 01.1	02.0	78 58.8	22.4	168 31.2	31.3	161 36.3	21.0
06	114 13.8	308 00.8	N 7 01.0	94 02.1	N 5 22.3	183 33.4	S22 31.3	176 38.7	S21 20.9
07	129 16.3	323 00.4	6 59.9	109 05.3	22.1	198 35.6	31.2	191 41.1	20.9
08	144 18.7	338 00.1	58.9	124 08.6	22.0	213 37.8	31.2	206 43.5	20.9
09	159 21.2	352 59.7 ..	57.8	139 11.8 ..	21.9	228 40.0 ..	31.2	221 45.9 ..	20.9
10	174 23.7	7 59.4	56.8	154 15.1	21.7	243 42.2	31.1	236 48.3	20.9
11	189 26.1	22 59.0	55.7	169 18.4	21.6	258 44.4	31.1	251 50.7	20.9
12	204 28.6	37 58.7	N 6 54.7	184 21.6	N 5 21.4	273 46.6	S22 31.1	266 53.0	S21 20.9
13	219 31.1	52 58.3	53.6	199 24.9	21.3	288 48.8	31.0	281 55.4	20.9
14	234 33.5	67 58.0	52.6	214 28.1	21.2	303 51.0	31.0	296 57.8	20.9
15	249 36.0	82 57.6 ..	51.6	229 31.4 ..	21.0	318 53.2 ..	31.0	312 00.2 ..	20.9
16	264 38.4	97 57.3	50.5	244 34.7	20.9	333 55.4	30.9	327 02.6	20.8
17	279 40.9	112 57.0	49.5	259 37.9	20.8	348 57.6	30.9	342 05.0	20.8
18	294 43.4	127 56.6	N 6 48.4	274 41.2	N 5 20.6	3 59.8	S22 30.9	357 07.4	S21 20.8
19	309 45.8	142 56.3	47.4	289 44.4	20.5	19 02.0	30.8	12 09.8	20.8
20	324 48.3	157 55.9	46.3	304 47.7	20.3	34 04.2	30.8	27 12.2	20.8
21	339 50.8	172 55.6 ..	45.2	319 50.9 ..	20.2	49 06.4 ..	30.8	42 14.6 ..	20.8
22	354 53.2	187 55.2	44.2	334 54.2	20.0	64 08.6	30.7	57 17.0	20.8
23	9 55.7	202 54.9	43.1	349 57.4	19.9	79 10.8	30.7	72 19.4	20.8

THURSDAY

STARS

Name	SHA	Dec
Acamar	315 14.0	S40 13.2
Achernar	335 22.3	S57 07.9
Acrux	173 04.4	S63 12.6
Adhara	255 08.5	S28 59.8
Aldebaran	290 43.3	N16 33.0
Alioth	166 16.7	N55 51.0
Alkaid	152 55.3	N49 12.8
Al Na'ir	27 37.0	S46 51.8
Alnilam	275 43.1	S 1 11.3
Alphard	217 51.3	S 8 44.7
Alphecca	126 07.0	N26 39.0
Alpheratz	357 38.0	N29 12.4
Altair	62 03.3	N 8 55.6
Ankaa	353 10.2	S42 11.7
Antares	112 20.3	S26 28.5
Arcturus	145 51.4	N19 04.7
Atria	107 18.0	S69 03.9
Avior	234 16.2	S59 34.2
Bellatrix	278 26.4	N 6 22.1
Betelgeuse	270 55.7	N 7 24.7
Canopus	263 59.7	S52 42.1
Capella	280 26.7	N46 00.9
Deneb	49 28.0	N45 21.5
Denebola	182 28.8	N14 27.6
Diphda	348 50.5	S17 52.4
Dubhe	193 45.9	N61 38.3
Elnath	278 06.0	N28 37.4
Eltanin	90 44.0	N51 29.5
Enif	33 42.0	N 9 58.3
Fomalhaut	15 18.1	S29 30.8
Gacrux	171 55.9	S57 13.5
Gienah	175 47.4	S17 39.2
Hadar	148 41.4	S60 28.2
Hamal	327 54.7	N23 33.6
Kaus Aust.	83 37.2	S34 21.3
Kochab	137 21.1	N74 04.4
Markab	13 33.1	N15 19.1
Menkar	314 09.5	N 4 10.3
Menkent	148 02.0	S36 28.1
Miaplacidus	221 39.2	S69 47.8
Mirfak	308 32.7	N49 55.9
Nunki	75 52.1	S26 16.2
Peacock	53 11.1	S56 40.3
Pollux	243 21.6	N27 58.3
Procyon	244 54.4	N 5 10.4
Rasalhague	96 01.9	N12 32.9
Regulus	207 38.3	N11 52.1
Rigel	281 07.0	S 8 10.6
Rigil Kent.	139 48.6	S60 55.1
Sabik	102 06.9	S15 44.9
Schedar	349 34.3	N56 39.1
Shaula	96 18.5	S37 05.8
Sirius	258 29.2	S16 44.5
Spica	158 26.3	S11 15.7
Suhail	222 48.9	S43 30.6
Vega	80 35.7	N38 48.5
Zuben'ubi	137 00.1	S16 07.6

	SHA	Mer. Pass.
Venus	193 56.4	
Mars	340 02.5	23 38
Jupiter	69 14.8	17 41
Saturn	62 23.6	18 08

Mer. Pass. 22 16.5 | v −0.3 d 1.1 | v 3.3 d 0.1 | v 2.2 d 0.0 | v 2.4 d 0.0

202   2020 OC

FRIDAY · SATURDAY

UT	ARIES GHA	VENUS −4.0 GHA	Dec
d h			
15 00	23 59.0	218 02.9	N 7 07.2
01	39 01.5	233 02.5	06.2
02	54 03.9	248 02.2	05.2
03	69 06.4	263 01.8 ..	04.1
04	84 08.9	278 01.5	03.1
05	99 11.3	293 01.1	02.0
06	114 13.8	308 00.8	N 7 01.0
07	129 16.3	323 00.4	6 59.9
08	144 18.7	338 00.1	58.9
09	159 21.2	352 59.7 ..	57.8
10	174 23.7	7 59.4	56.8
11	189 26.1	22 59.0	55.7
12	204 28.6	37 58.7	N 6 54.7
13	219 31.1	52 58.3	53.6
14	234 33.5	67 58.0	52.6
15	249 36.0	82 57.6 ..	51.6
16	264 38.4	97 57.3	50.5

NAUTICAL ALMANAC, VENUS & SIRIUS

FIG. 16

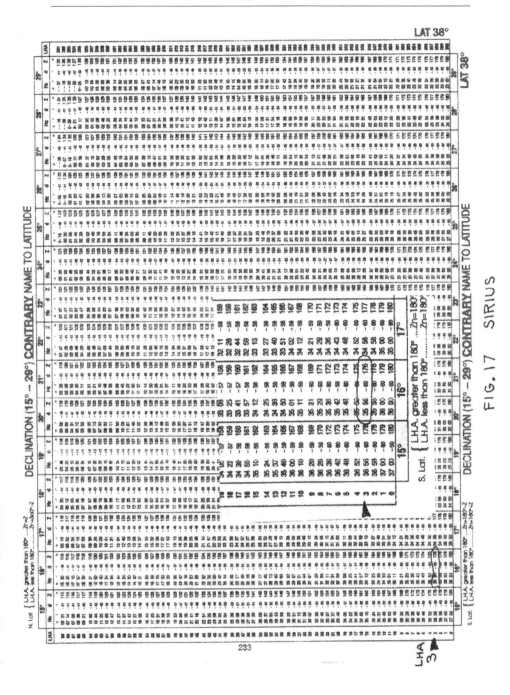

FIG. 17 SIRIUS

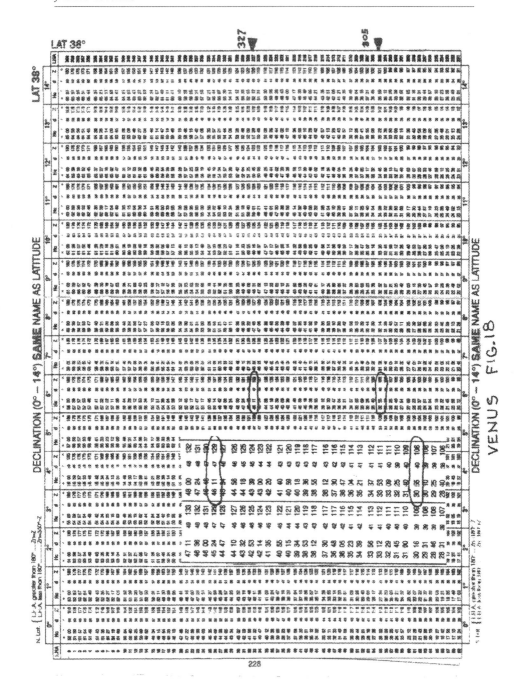

VENUS FIG. 18

SIRIUS   15 OCT, 2020   DR 38N, 123W

NAUTICAL TWILIGHT   05:13   ASM LAT 38N
SUNRISE   06:12   ASM LONG 123:01.6

EST TIME OF SIGHT   05:32   PLOT FROM (AP)
ADD ZONE 8   + 8:00   ASSUMED POSITION
                     13:32

GHA SIRIUS = GHA ARIES + SHA SIRIUS
NAUTICAL ALMANAC: PG 202, FIG. 16

UT (GMT)   GHA
            ARIES

13:00   219:31.1

  32   8:01.3   (INCREMENTS & CORRECTIONS PG XVII)
13:32   227:32.4 = GHA ARIES
              +
SHA SIRIUS 258:29.2   DEC SIRIUS = S16:44.5
GHA SIRIUS = 485:61.6 = 486:01.6   363   45
−ASM LONGITUDE   − 123:01.6   −360
  LHA   363   3
                                    LHA = 003

  ENTER HO 249, PG 233   LAT   LHA   NAME   DEC
                          38   003   CONTRARY   16

  HO 249 RESULT: H_c d   z   HO 249
                  35:56   −60   176   TABLE 5

IF LHA LESS THAN 180 ∴ $Z_n = 360 - Z$ ÷45
           360
          −176
           184   Zn = 184

H_c = 35:56   CONSTRUCTED H_o = 35:14
        −45 H_c = 35:11
       35:11   3

                        Z_n = 184 T 3

COAST GUARD ACADEMY (C GREATER AWAY) (H_c LESS = T)

FIG. 19

$\boxed{\text{VENUS}}$

13 OCT, 2020

SUNRISE: 06:12

D.R. 38N, 123W

A.P. 38N, 122:58W

PICK SIGHT TIME: 06:00 PST

FOR ZONE 8,   + 8:00
UT(GMT) =   14:00

UT	GHA VENUS	DEC
14:00	067:58.0	N6:52.6

+ 360

427:58.0

-122:58 (MINUS ASM LONG FOR WHOLE ✳ LHA)

LHA = 305

ENTER HO 249 TABLES, PG 228 (FIG. 18):

LAT	LHA	NAME	DEC	RESULT:	Hc	d	Z
38	305	SAME	N6		30:55	40	108

IF LHA GREATER THAN 180 ··· $Z_n = Z$ ∴ $Z_n = 108$

SCAN TABLES FOR Z = 129 (OUR PHYSICAL REQUIREMENT)

LAT	LHA	NAME	DEC	RESULT:	Hc	d	Z
38	327	SAME	6°		46:11	47	129

LHA = 327, Z = 129

IF LHA GREATER THAN 180 ··· $Z_n = Z$

COAST GUARD ACADEMY = Hc GREATER THAN Ho, = AWAY(A)

CONSTRUCT FOR EASY PLOT: Ho 46:13
                            Hc 46:11
                                 02

FROM OUR KNOWN POSITION: $Z_n = 129$, TZ

FIG. 20

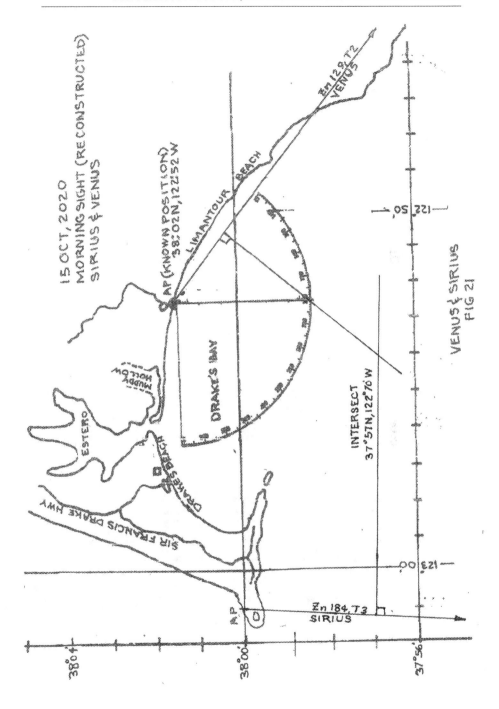

15 OCT, 2020
MORNING SIGHT (RECONSTRUCTED)
SIRIUS ¢ VENUS

AP (KNOWN POSITION)
38:02N, 122:52 W

LIMANTOUR BEACH

Zn 12.9, T2
VENUS

DRAKE'S BAY

MURPHY HOLLOW

ESTERO

DRAKE'S BEACH

SIR FRANCIS DRAKE HWY

INTERSECT
37°57N, 122°76 W

122°50'

VENUS ¢ SIRIUS
FIG 21

123°00

AP

Zn 184, T3
SIRIUS

37°56

38°04

38°00

∴ d°CORRECTION MAY BE ENTERED FROM TOP OR SIDE WITH SAM RESULTS
TABLE 5 (HO 249) FIG. 22

CHAPTER 8

SUNDIAL----COPPERHENGE

The sundial represents the first clock of civilization. It is my goal to help you build one for yourself that will not only keep accurate time, but will also allow you to track the ANALEMMA. In addition, it will allow you to mark the angular range of sunrise for your latitude. This scientific data collection device, which I named COPPERHENGE, built on a larger scale, provided the information needed to determine our elliptical orbit around the sun.

The first step is to select a spot in your garden that receives maximum sun during the day. Select a birdbath for the pedestal, mine is an attractive lime green. The pedestal requires a permanent mount. Create a level spot approximately 20 x 20 inches square. Construct a frame 20 x 20 x 4 inches high for the ready-mix concrete base. This will require about 4 bags of mix.

Bird bathes usually come in two pieces, a bowl and a stand. If yours has a removable bowl and a hollow stand, you will need to make a hole in the bowl for a secure attachment. Place the bowl bottom down on solid concrete. While maintaining contact with the bowl and the concrete and using a large steel bolt or drift pin, gently hammer the pin into the center of the bowl. Soon the bottom will begin to crumble. Make the hole 50% larger than the hollow hole in the base. The larger hole allows room for the forming of small diameter re-bar for the attachment.

Slowly mix the concrete in a wheel barrow using a hoe, one bag at a time. Measure out the suggested quantity of water. Be very stingy with the water in the beginning. When the form is filled and is firm enough to support the stand, insert the first piece of re-bar. The re-bar should be no more than 4 feet in length and have a 2-inch right angle bend to enable solid connection with the base. One 8-foot piece of 3/8 re-bar, cut in half should suffice.

Note: For best results, cut and form the rebar before final insertion. The finished job requires keeping the rebar below the top of the bowl, making the bowl sit level, filling the pedestal shaft, and finally filling the bowl. For best results keep the job wetted down for at least one day.

Now for the fun part. You will need sheet copper with a minimum thickness of 1/16 inch. 2 millimeters or 3/32 of an inch is much better. The completed device will require 2 each, 16-inch square sheets plus an additional half sheet, 8 x 16, for the GNOMON and anathema plate.

WARNING: THIS JOB REQUIRES SOLDERING*******SOLDERING REQUIRES EYE PROTECTION! DO NOT ATTEMPT ANY SOLDER JOINT WITHOUT EYEGLASSES, SAFETY GLASSES OR A SAFETY SHIELD.

Carefully locate the hole in the center of the first sheet. The finished hole should be a tight ¼ inch but use a slightly smaller hole for now. The best idea is to drill and tap for a ¼ -20 brass round head machine screw. Run the screw up from underneath and later solder it in place. For a rigid compass, use a wood strip with a ¼ inch hole at one end and a finishing nail spaced 8 inches away. the holes matched for a tight fit with the screw and nail.

The job requires marking and cutting 2 each, 16-inch circles. I recommend scoring the sheets with a second circle, 1/16 of an inch outside as a guide for accurate cutting. Now score one of the large circles with a 12-inch diameter inner circle and using the same technique as above, cut this piece to form a 2-inch-wide ring with a 12- inch inner circle. Here you will need to decide how much work you want to do. Either make a curving cut with the saw blade from the outside edge to the 12-inch inner circle or create a slot for starting the saw blade. For the slot I suggest drilling a close pattern of 1/16 inch holes, then opening this into the slot. If you take the easy way, the cut will not be visible because it will be covered over with the hour plate.

PROJECT OVERVIEW: The construction goal is to locate the assembly on a NORTH/ SOUTH (N/S) line. You will initially construct the unit with a N/S line, then when complete, align it with true NORTH.

Clean up all cuts with a file and sandpaper. The inner circle is the rotatable sundial base. The ring is attached to the largebase circle with rivets, solder or both. Locate 3 holes, 120 degrees apart on an 8 5/8 bolt circle. The holes will fit 10-32 brass studs which will be embedded into the pedestal.

Mark and drill a hole in the south point of the assembly, on a 7- inch radius. Locate and drill two more identical holes, 120 degrees apart. Place the disk in the center of the pedestal. Using your most precise method, with the copper disk centered, your job is to get as close as possible in the initial setup to locate north.

Methods to determine N/S are an ordinary magnetic compass with a known deviation, an app on a cell phone or computer, a known parallel line, transferred from a nearby building, or a sight on Polaris. I used the computer ap with the computer raised up on boxes to a height even with the pedestal. I then drilled a ¼ -inch hole near the end of a yardstick. Laying the yardstick over both the disk center and the computer screen, I was able to set up the N/S line with the yardstick center Later I had to readjust it slightly.

Locate and drill the holes for 10-32 x 3-inch brass mounting studs. The studs should be secured to the disk with nuts on both sides. Secure the studs to the pedestal with epoxy, or better yet, a small bit of intentionally leftover ready-mix concrete. When dry, cut down the studs to fit mounting nuts. I used special round headed brass acorn nuts.

The GNOMON (crazy spelling, pronounced NO MEN), is custom set to your actual latitude. In my case the angle is 38 degrees. At this point, everything is in a state of flux and this is where the builder must determine the geometry of his own project. For the prototype, I elected to construct a removable GNOMEN, in case I had a better idea in the future. I made a base plate, 2 inches wide x 6 ½ inches long. I drilled a ¼ inch hole inside one end. The slope of the 38-degree GNOMEN begins at the center of the sundial. Based on experimentation with an earlier version, I decided to shorten the base length from the hole center to 4 ¾ inches. On June 21, the sun will project a shadow about ½ inch from the vertical front edge. My prototype unit is soldered to the plate. For strength and to assist with alignment. The base of the unit has 2 tabs which fit into holes in the base plate. In addition, the slope is reinforced with a slotted angle piece near the end, see diagram. The assembly will take some time, be as precise as possible. I clamped the slope on a drill press base and the base plate was free to move around under the tabs before soldering. I attached my gnomon with 2 studs. The base of the slope must be cut away to make room for a flat washer and nut.

I built a second sundial for my friend Eric. It is a much simpler design, with the gnomon soldered directly to the disk. It incorporates two tabs which fit into two alignment holes.

My design requires constructing a curved dial plate, fitted over the outer ring. The plate comes within a ¼ inch from the base of the GNOMEN. The advantage of the removable dial plate is that it allows for easier marking of the roman numerals and hour lines. Also, it is reversable, just in case you need be more precise the second time. When the shadows are short, the tip of the gnomon will fall inside the dial plate.

The analemma backing plate is attached with the same two screws which attach the dial plate. These holes require precision locating. On the base plate disk, scribe a line from the disk center across the 2-inch rim. This will become the N/S line. Using your MARKING STRIP with a finishing nail, 7 inches from the center, scribe an arc, 2-inches each way from the line center. Drill 3 small (1/16 inch) holes for a close fit with a small finishing nail (ref FIG 24). Center and clamp the HOUR PLATE to the disk. Flip the assembly over and match drill the center hole to the HOUR PLATE. Remove the hour plate, center and match drill the analemma plate. Drill and tap the two outer holes of the assembly for 8-32 threads. If you need to be more precise, you can readjust the holes for 10-32 threads. On the finished unit, use a brass nail attached to a small chain to lock in N/S.

HOUR MARKING:

Do not be in a rush to mark the hour lines, be precise and let the sun work for you. Read these three entire paragraphs several times before starting. The sun will be on your meridian, four different times in the year. The two seasons of minimal change are SPRING and SUMMER. Fall and winter move much faster. My best idea is to mark the hour lines between the dates of the vernal equinox and the end of summer, when the sun is on N/S. Refer to your ALMANAC, the SUN is on your N/S MERIDIAN, 15 APR, 12 JUN, 1 SEP. Note, the other date the sun is on your N/S meridian is 25 DEC. This date is not good for marking hour lines but is the best day for aligning the assembly.

The first step for hour marking is to make sure the assembly is aligned N/S. This will be the Local Apparent Noon and the 12- hour mark. Once satisfied, with the SUN on the LAN noon line, wait exactly one hour from the LAN time to mark the next hour line. Be sure that the dial does not rotate during the marking. A simple marking method is to use a prick punch, then circle the spot with a marking pen. Continue marking as long as the GNOMON can cast a shadow. Early the next morning, continue marking with the same LAN time offset until reaching noon for a check.

Scribe the hour lines with the tool that you created (FIG XX). Remove the rotatable disk. Place the tool on the center stud of the dial and using the back edge of an EXACTO KNIFE or similar sharp instrument. Inscribe a line from each hour dot across the dial plate, edge to edge Take your time, try to avoid scratching outside the line. Mistakes can be removed with fine sandpaper. Once you are satisfied with the hour lines, make a layout sketch of the ROMAN NUMERAL marking.

If you can rent, borrow, or buy a roman numeral set, that would be ideal. If not, you can use a ½ inch wide chisel and create your own. Practice marking on a piece of scrap. Use your hour marking tool for a compass and with appropriate nail holes, create guide lines for the numerals. Scribe a light arc ¼- inch from the outside border of the dial plate then another inside to fit the numerals. Remove the hour plate and place it on a hard flat surface for the marking.

ANALEMMA MARKING:

I use a prick punch, a handy spring-loaded tool, used to locate hole centers for sheet metal work. The advantage of this tool is that it requires only one hand and makes a consistent mark. I soldered a thin 4-inch x 12-inch brass plate on top of the removable analemma plate to mark the track of the analemma. I use a notebook in conjunction with the NAUTICAL ALMANAC

The righthand page of the almanac lists the sun movements and covers a three-day period. At the bottom of the page is the EQUATION OF TIME, listed for the period. This lists the minutes and seconds of the meridian crossing difference throughout the year. The range is -14 minutes to +16 minutes, negative times are shaded. I am located in zone 8, 8 hours after GREENWICH. There are two listings, 12 hours apart with a range of about 10 seconds. 8 hours is 2/3 of 12 hours. I multiply the difference in seconds times 0.7 and add or subtract as required.

You must determine the exact time the sun will cross your meridian. The sun travels 15 degrees per hour or 1 degree per 4 minutes. Zone 8 is centered at 120 degrees, the vertical boundary between California and Nevada. Making use of my GPS longitude and time to arc distance calculations from the NAUTICAL ALMANAC, and from a chart, I have determined that my longitude, 122:45 equals 11 minutes and 26 seconds past 120 degrees. This is when the perfect sun crosses my meridian, 8 hours, 11 minutes and 26 seconds after GREENWICH. This is also noted as LOCAL APPARENT NOON (LAN).

On the left page of the note book, I add or subtract the results of the NAUTICAL ALMANAC to my constant, 8:11:26. Note that 8:10: 86 is the same thing. On the right-hand side of the note book I enter the date, the offset and the result.

I rotate the dial until the shadow shows parallel lines, pay particular attention to the shadow nearest the gnomon. At the precise moment of the calculated time, I place a punch mark at the end of the GNOMEN'S shadow and place a tiny circle around it with my marking pen. I then circle the result in the notebook. Anytime I am unable to complete the mark, I omit the circle. Because the changes are slow, do not create marks less than a week apart. Try to record special events like the equinoxes, solstices, the four times the sun is on the N/S line plus the crossover point. The exception is late December when there is maximum movement. Record every possible day between the 21st and the 30th. I am still pondering whether or not to rotate the disk for a straight, parallel shadow while the sun is in the northern hemisphere or just lock the disk on N/S. The difference is very slight. I did the rotation, but the lockdown advantage would result in a smoother track. Based on my experience, I suggest the easy way.

SUNRISE MARKING:

The sunrise occurs between four extreme angles, the dates are determined from the almanac. Mark and drill a small hole on the center of the outside ring at the sunrise occurrence points. Solder a brass nail to mark each spot. The nail should pin a date strip to the assembly. If you do not have a clear view of sunrise on that day, transfer the angle from another place. This could be measured from a window, the edge of a building, or some other appropriate surface.

USING YOUR CUSTOM SUNDIAL:

At 12 noon on your watch, rotate the dial until the gnomon shadow matches the time. You can now read real time on your new instrument. This will be most accurate for 3 hours before and after noon. March through September will demonstrate most accuracy. The shadows will track very closely with your watch. You can even scribe ¼ and ½ -hour lines if you want. Have fun with your new instrument. ENJOY!

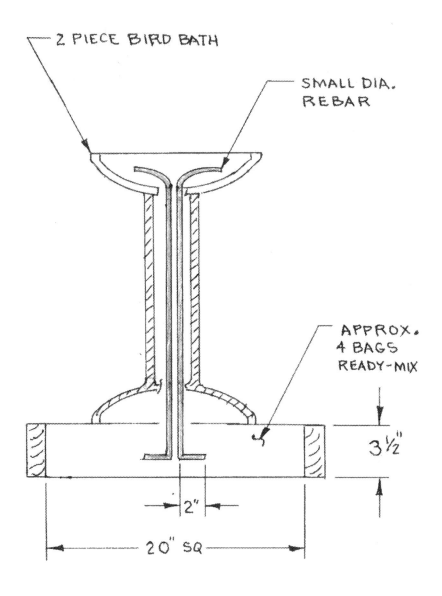

2 PIECE BIRD BATH

SMALL DIA. REBAR

APPROX. 4 BAGS READY-MIX

3½"

2"

20" SQ

FIG. 23

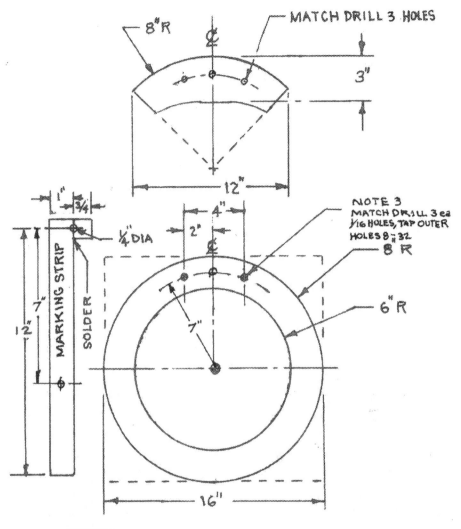

NOTE:
 1. CUT TWO 16" CIRCLES
 2. CUT 12" CIRCLE INSIDE SECOND CIRCLE
 3. LOCATE THE 1/16" HOLES WITH MAX. PRECISION
    MATCH DRILL ANALEMMA & HOUR PLATE
        FIG. 24

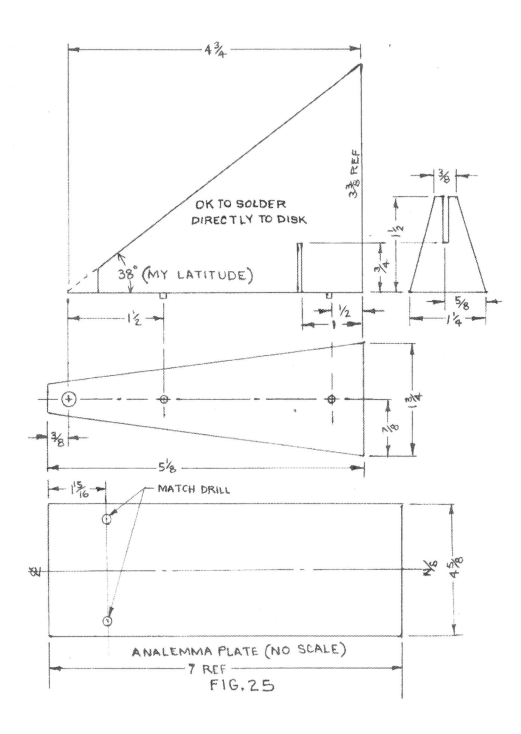

OK TO SOLDER DIRECTLY TO DISK

38° (MY LATITUDE)

4 3/4

3 3/8 REF

3/8

1/2

3/4

5/8

1 1/4

1 1/2

1/2

1 1/2

3/8

3/4

1/8

5/8

1 5/16

MATCH DRILL

8

9/16

4 5/8

ANALEMMA PLATE (NO SCALE)

7 REF

FIG. 25

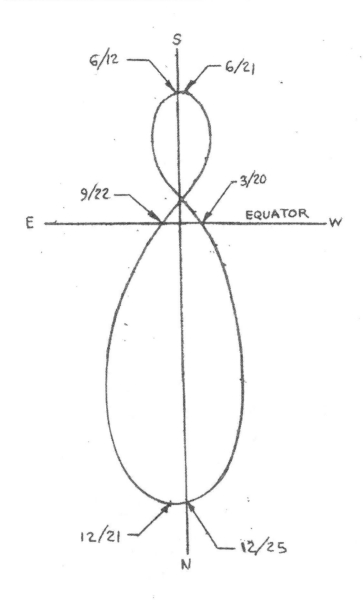

THE ANALEMMA
(SHADOW OF THE GNOMON)

FIG. 26

DEFINITIONS

GHA = Greenwich hour angle. The range of GHA is from 0 to 360 degrees. GHA begins at 000 on the Greenwich meridian increasing WESTWARD back to 360 at the Greenwich meridian.

SHA = sidereal hour angle. The range is 0 to 360 degrees.

DEC or Dec (preferred) = declination. The measured angle of the GP of the celestial object.

GP = geographical position. The location of the center to center line between a celestial object and earth where it passes through our planet's surface.

Long = longitude. The sign convention is: east is positive, west is negative. The range is -180 to + 180 degrees.

Lat = latitude. The sign convention is: north is positive, south is negative. The range is -90 to + 90 degrees.

LHA = GHA + Long = local hour angle. The LHA increases to the west from 0 on the local meridian to 360 degrees.

Hc = calculated altitude.

Hs = sextant altitude.

Ho = observed altitude.

Z = Zn = true azimuth. Z is measured from true north through east, south, west and back to north. The range is from 0 to 360 degrees.

Ie = sextant index error.

DIP = dip of horizon.

NOTE: Unless you are located on your MERIDIAN, a GREAT
          CIRCLE directly overhead {ZENITH) that passes through
          both N and S poles, a sextant measurement will place you on
          a circle of equal altitudes, AKA, a circle of equal angles, also
          known as a GREAT CIRCLE.

From HO-249:

Assumed LATITUDE: The latitude closest to your position. The
difference is resolved with the plot.

Assumed LONGITUDE: A whole number in degrees to allow entry
into the table. The difference between this and your actual position is
resolved using TABLE 5.

SAME NAME: The GP is located in your hemisphere.

CONTRARY NAME: The GP is not located in your hemisphere.

BIBLIOGRAPHY

Read, James, CURIOSITY, ADVENTURE TRAVEL, EXPLORATION, TRADE, WAR, MURDER: THE EUROPEAN EXPANSION, 15TH TO 20TH CENTURY
Amazon Create Space, 2021
Lulu Publishing Service, 2019

Howse, Derek, Greenwich time and the discovery of the longitude Oxford University Press, 1980

Excerpts by permission:

NATIONAL IMAGERY AND MAPPING AGENCY, SIGHT REDUCTION TABLES for AIR NAVAGATION, LATITUDES 0 -40 Degrees, DECLINATIONS 0 – 29 Degrees, PUB NO 249, VOLUME 2 (HO-249)
Celestaire Inc, Commercial Edition

NAUTICAL ALMANAC, 2021 COMMERCIAL EDITION
Celestaire Inc, Commercial Edition
Permission from UK Hydrographic Office, 2022

Printed in the United States
by Baker & Taylor Publisher Services